100 Ideas for Early Years Practitioners:

Forest School

Other titles in the 100 Ideas for Early Years Practitioners series:

100 Ideas for Early Years Practitioners: Outstanding Practice
by Lucy Peet

100 Ideas for Early Years Practitioners: School Readiness
by Claire Ford

100 Ideas for Early Years Practitioners: Outdoor Play
by Julie Mountain

100 Ideas for Early Years Practitioners: Supporting EAL Learners
by Marianne Sargent

Coming soon:

100 Ideas for Early Years Practitioners: Observation, Assessment and Planning
by Marianne Sargent

100 Ideas for Early Years Practitioners:

Forest School

Tracey Maciver

BLOOMSBURY
LONDON • OXFORD • NEW YORK • NEW DELHI • SYDNEY

Bloomsbury Education
An imprint of Bloomsbury Publishing Plc

50 Bedford Square	1385 Broadway
London	New York
WC1B 3DP	NY 10018
UK	USA

www.bloomsbury.com

BLOOMSBURY and the Diana logo are trademarks of
Bloomsbury Publishing Plc

First published in Great Britain 2018

Copyright © Tracey Maciver, 2018

Tracey Maciver has asserted his/her right under the Copyright, Designs and Patents Act, 1988, to be identified as Author of this work.

All rights reserved. No part of this publication may be reproduced or transmitted in any form or by any means, electronic or mechanical, including photocopying, recording, or any information storage or retrieval system, without prior permission in writing from the publishers.

No responsibility for loss caused to any individual or organization acting on or refraining from action as a result of the material in this publication can be accepted by Bloomsbury or the author.

A catalogue record for this book is available from the British Library.

ISBN:
PB: 9781472946652
ePub: 9781472946638
ePDF: 9781472946669

2 4 6 8 10 9 7 5 3

Typeset by Newgen KnowledgeWorks Pvt. Ltd., Chennai, India
Printed and bound by CPI Group (UK) Ltd. Croydon, CR0 4YY

This book is produced using paper that is made from wood grown in managed, sustainable forests. It is natural, renewable and recyclable. The logging and manufacturing processes conform to the environmental regulations of the country of origin.

To find out more about our authors and books visit www.bloomsbury.com. Here you will find extracts, author interviews, details of forthcoming events and the option to sign up for our newsletters.

Contents

Acknowledgements	viii
Introduction	ix
How to use this book	x

Part 1: Getting ready — **1**

1. Preparing for the outdoors	2
2. What do we need to wear for Forest School?	3
3. What do I need to take with me?	4
4. Marking boundaries	6
5. Welly walk	7
6. Rope bus	8
7. Tree decorating	9
8. Books in the woods	10

Part 2: Using tools — **11**

9. Introducing using tools with young children	12
10. The rope safety circle	13
11. Low-risk tools	14
12. Whittling tools	15
13. Loppers and secateurs	16
14. Sawing tools	17
15. Drilling tools	18

Part 3: Fire — **19**

16. Getting ready for fire	20
17. How to light a fire	22
18. Making charcoal in a tin	23
19. Making firelighters	24
20. Fire words mobile	25
21. Campfire cookery	26
22. Bannock	28
23. Chapattis	29
24. Foil parcels	30
25. Nettle soup	31
26. Making popcorn	32

27	Roasting sweet chestnuts	33
28	Cooking with apples	34
29	Hot bananas	36

Part 4: Trees and leaves — **37**

30	Leaf sewing	38
31	Hessian pictures	39
32	Colour postcards	40
33	Autumn leaf spiral mobile	41
34	Autumn leaf wreath	42
35	Leaf fishing	43
36	Leaf masks for forest superheroes	44
37	Woodland magic	45
38	Conker balance	46
39	Acorn mushrooms	47
40	Sycamore seed crafts	48
41	Christmas tree crafts	49
42	Nature plaques	50
43	Elder beads	51
44	Leaf ID bunting	52
45	Tree cookie blackboards	53
46	Willow domes	54
47	Sunflower dens	55
48	Growing trees	56

Part 5: Sticks and plants — **57**

49	Tree cookies	58
50	Bell shaker	59
51	Simple dreamcatchers	60
52	Log houses	61
53	Elder bubble wands	62
54	Fairy doors	63
55	Willow lanterns	64
56	Forest friends and mini dens	66
57	Marionette puppets	68

Part 6: Bugs and minibeasts — **69**

58	Umbrella bug-catching	70
59	Peg caterpillars	71
60	Butterfly petal-bashing	72
61	Threading caterpillars	73
62	Snail racing	74
63	Bug stones	75
64	Sticky spider's web	76

Part 7: Mud and weather — **77**
- 65 Making mud paint — 78
- 66 Mud painting — 79
- 67 Mud bricks — 80
- 68 Pitter patter flood! — 81
- 69 Rain painting — 82
- 70 Rainstorm music — 83
- 71 Wind drawing — 84
- 72 Wind streamers — 85
- 73 Kites — 86
- 74 Experimenting with ice — 87
- 75 Ice windows — 88
- 76 Snow paths — 89

Part 8: Wildlife — **91**
- 77 Animal ears — 92
- 78 Animal games — 93
- 79 Pine cone hedgehogs — 94
- 80 Animal tracks — 95
- 81 Stone and leaf animals — 96
- 82 Fluffy owlets — 97
- 83 Birds' nests — 98
- 84 Festive bird garlands — 99
- 85 Orange bird feeders — 100
- 86 Apple bird feeders — 101

Part 9: Adventures of the imagination — **103**
- 87 Dinosaur bone hunt — 104
- 88 Salt dough leaf fossils — 105
- 89 Story stones — 106
- 90 Barefoot walk — 107
- 91 Smelly trails — 108
- 92 Forest pets — 109
- 93 Gold rush — 110
- 94 Shadows — 111
- 95 Den building — 112
- 96 Body art — 113
- 97 Gross motor playground — 114
- 98 Forest School in the dark — 115
- 99 The unplanned adventure — 116
- 100 Reviewing the session — 117

Further reading — 118

Acknowledgements

Thank you for reading this book. I would like to thank Davy for his support and encouragement, Cat Maciver for looking after Dan while I got on with the writing process, and the students and children I have encountered and worked with, who were willing to try out all the activities. I would also like to thank Alan Dyer and Gordon Woodall for introducing me to Forest School many years ago.

Introduction

Forest School is not a new concept. It originated in Scandinavia in the 1950s and was intended as a means to teach children about the natural world and environmental issues. By the 1980s, Forest School had become a significant part of the Scandinavian preschool programme for under sevens. Forest School stems from the Swedish 'småbørnspædagogik', or Early Years education, and focuses on learning by experience. It was first introduced to Britain by Bridgwater College in 1993 and has since been developed into a learning concept for children from Early Years through to young people with low self-esteem and challenging behaviour.

Rather than concentrating on academic skills, the Forest School approach is more focused on helping to develop personal, social and emotional skills such as self-discovery, confidence and independence, as well as encouraging communication skills and raising self-esteem. Children visit woodlands or natural outdoor areas and learn through play how to cooperate and work with others to solve problems, use their own initiative and handle risks. Building self-esteem is at the core of the Forest School ethos, along with raising emotional awareness and confidence, encouraging independence and providing opportunities for active outdoor play and discovery, with deep-level and memorable learning experiences.

All of these 'soft skills' are transferable back into the nursery setting and beyond. They are skills that the child can use to build their resilience and character throughout the rest of their life.

The Forest School Association, which is a collection of Forest School leaders and interested parties dedicated to promoting Forest School in the UK, introduced an ethos in 2011 of six principles and criteria for good practice. These are available to view on their website www.forestschoolassociation.org.

How to use this book

This book includes quick, easy, practical ideas and guidance for you to dip in and out of, to help you plan and carry out Forest School activities for the children in your care.

Each idea includes:

- a catchy title, easy to refer to and share with your colleagues
- a quote from a practitioner, parent or child describing their experience that has led to the idea
- a summary of the idea in bold, making it easy to flick through the book and identify an idea you want to use at a glance
- a step-by-step guide to implementing the idea.

Each idea also includes one or more of the following:

Teaching tip
Practical tips and advice for how and how not to run the activity or put the idea into practice.

Taking it further
Ideas and advice for how to extend the idea or develop it further.

Bonus idea ★
There are 51 bonus ideas in this book that are extra exciting, extra original and extra interesting.

Involving parents
Tips for how to get parents involved in their child's learning, either in the early years setting or at home.

Share how you use these ideas and find out what other practitioners have done using **#100ideas**.

Getting ready

Part 1

IDEA 1

Preparing for the outdoors

'What do I need to prepare for Forest School sessions?'

Even if you are planning to carry out a session that is child-led with free play using only natural resources that you find, you still need to prepare for the session. Before taking the children to the woods, you need to plan for success.

Making sure that you are prepared for anything will build your confidence and professional practice.

- Risk assess and check the area prior to children visiting. Make sure that it is suitable for the activities you have in mind, it is litter- and debris-free and you are aware of anything that could pose a risk.
- Rather than removing every danger, enable children to learn how to manage risks themselves as part of the learning process. Make them aware of hazards.
- Reinforce boundaries and where children can go during the session.
- Continually monitor safety in the area. Do not undertake sessions in woodlands or under trees when there are strong winds, due to the risk of falling branches.
- Risk-assess the journey to the outdoor area. Think about a rope bus (see Idea 6) and some golden rules.
- Make sure that you are well prepared, including first aid kits, a working telephone with emergency contacts, and up-to-date information about the children (and/or adults) in your group with regard to allergies and medical needs.
- If you are working in woodlands rather than on nursery grounds, have a map reference of where you are and entry points for vehicles.
- Enlist sufficient adults to cover your ratios.

Teaching tip

Have a Forest School grab-bag for every session with a first aid kit, phone and important information. Make sure that your first aid kit is fully stocked and in date. Some spare clothes like hats, gloves and raincoats would be a good addition.

Taking it further

I cannot recommend taking an outdoor first aid course highly enough. It will give you the knowledge and confidence to deliver emergency first aid outdoors.

IDEA 2

What do we need to wear for Forest School?

'Whatever the weather, don't forget your wellies!'

It is important to make sure that each member of your group is dressed adequately for whatever the weather can throw at you during that session.

There is nothing worse than being outside, cold, wet and miserable, to dampen the enthusiasm for learning and exploring. Start as you mean to go on.

- Check that everybody in your group is suitably dressed to spend the session outside.
- If it is cold, do they have enough clothes and layers? Layers of clothing made of natural fibres, such as cotton and wool, provide more insulation than man-made materials. Do they have warm coats, hats and gloves and thick socks to wear?
- On a wet day, waterproof outer clothing and footwear are required.
- Hot days will require suitable clothing that will keep children cool but still protect them from scratches and stings that happen when outside. Long sleeves and trousers are a good idea. Sturdy shoes, trainers or wellies will protect feet from prickles or stings. Are they wearing sun cream and a hat to help prevent sunburn?
- When checking clothing, also make sure that the adults are appropriately dressed. Some nurseries supply coats and waterproof trousers for staff and visitors. An uncomfortable adult will not give their best or want to participate in an extended period outdoors if they are wet or cold.

Teaching tip

Pair welly boots and hold together with clothes pegs, labelled with names or sizes. If you have room, make a shoe rack by drilling a whole at each end of a plank of wood. Thread rope handles through the holes and insert doweling rods into the plank at intervals to store inverted boots. This is a great way of taking wellies to your changing area and allowing them to dry afterwards.

Involving parents

In the classroom, you can display images or even a child-sized mannequin of appropriate clothes for being outdoors, so that parents can see exactly the types of clothing that are suitable for your sessions. Set up an outgrown collection point for waterproofs and wellies. Many parents will not mind donating outgrown items if you ask.

IDEA 3

What do I need to take with me?

'I'm always afraid I'll forget something vital or the session won't work because the children are not engaged.'

Having all the resources you need with you ready for the session will ensure that you can complete the activities you have planned during your time outside.

When planning your session, it is a good idea to include a checklist of everything you need to take with you, to make sure that nothing gets left behind.

- Make sure that you have all the resources you will need to complete each activity you have planned and that you have enough for the size of the group that you have. Remember to include a few extras in case of damages, mistakes or adults wishing to take part too.
- Always overprepare and have a spare activity or two. If something does not work well, don't flog a dead horse; move on to the next thing. If you finish an activity more quickly than you thought you would, you need to have something extra to fill the gap. This could be a game or activity that does not require any resources.
- Be prepared to change your session plan to fit in with the needs of the group or unexpected changes in the weather. Outdoor learning is sometimes unpredictable but can offer new learning opportunities for both your group and yourself. If it is wet and slippery, a running game is probably not a good idea; if it is windy, a quiet listening game will be quite challenging; and if it is swelteringly hot, do children want to be heaving heavy sticks to make shelters?

Teaching tip

The best sessions in my experience have not been those that have gone completely to plan, but those that embrace learning opportunities as they present themselves. Learning opportunities appear more often when you follow the children's lead. If the session ends up with your planned activity staying in your bag, because the children have been totally engaged in their own agenda, playing, cooperating and extending their own and each other's learning, that is a successful session.

- If you are using a campfire for your session, make sure that the fire is always attended by a reliable adult and keep plenty of water to hand to douse both the fire and any person who may burn themselves. A bucket of water to plunge hands into is always a good idea, with an old towel soaking in it to be used as a fire blanket if needed.
- A good outdoor session will consist of a mixture of activities and games, as well as child-led learning and free play. Think about the learning outcomes you want to achieve or the areas of learning you want to cover, and provide resources and activities accordingly.
- Take water to drink and the means to make a hot drink if you are outside when it is cold, whether that is materials to make a fire, a storm kettle or a flask of hot water. Warm hot chocolate, warm diluted juice syrups (available from health food shops or the baby section of supermarkets) or fruit tea bags (use the sort that does not contain tea) are some of the warm drinks you may want to try.
- If you are outside for an extended period, make sure that you take snacks to revitalise everyone when they are flagging. What sort of snacks do you have in nursery? Prepare them in advance or take snacks that require no preparation – for example, cut fruit, rice cakes, breadsticks or biscuits.
- Hygiene when outside is as important as when you are in the nursery. A pack of wet wipes and a bin bag are vital to take with you at all times when out and about. Handwashing after toileting and before snacks can be achieved by transporting a container of water to your site, along with hand soap and hand towels. I use a solar shower hung from a branch, as these have an on/off tap. They are available from most camping shops or online.

> **Bonus idea** ★
>
> I usually take a resources bag with me to enhance children's play and their own projects. This includes balls of string, scissors, pens, postcards, a ball, some rope, a small tarpaulin or two, magnifying glasses, collecting pots and identification charts. As I observe children's play over the sessions, I may add some additional resources in line with group or individual interests, such as animal finger puppets, model fairies, wooden cars or dinosaurs. Some light material such as old net curtains or large head scarves can also be a welcome addition to extend play sessions.

IDEA 4

Marking boundaries

'I worry that the children will wander off and get lost, as we use a large woodland which is a few minutes' walk from our nursery.'

Setting boundaries with young children is important. Talk about staying within sight of the adults but be open to allowing them to decide on how far they should go.

Many adults worry about the worst-case scenario of losing a child in the woods but, in reality, if boundaries are set, children are very eager to show responsibility and follow your lead.

- Before children visit the site, check the area for anything that could pose a significant hazard, such as open water, a sheer drop or a tree with unsafe branches. Rope these areas off.
- Find a stick about the height of your shortest child and pop a hat on it. Stick it into the ground at various places around your site, go back to the central point and check whether you can see it. This should give you a good indication as to where your boundaries should be.
- When the children are in the woods, ask them how far they think they should go. For the first few sessions, they will opt to stay in quite a confined space.
- Give the children some bright ribbon or material and help them fix it to trees to show how far they can go. If children set their own boundaries, they are more likely to stay within them.
- As the children become familiar with the site, they will want to extend the boundaries, so do not be worried about starting sessions in a small space. Set the boundaries session by session. By the time you get to the fifth session, many children will want to position their markers at the boundaries identified by the stick with a hat on it.

Teaching tip

Explore the Forest School area with the children on a welly walk (Idea 5) or using the rope bus (Idea 6), so they become familiar with their surroundings. Let the children take ownership of the space by letting them decide what each area is called. A class of reception children in Plymouth called a mound in their area 'Dead Man's Corner', which stuck and was used by children and teachers alike.

IDEA 5

Welly walk

'It's Wet Welly Wednesday. I wear welly boots all day!' Jack, aged four, Plymouth

Welly walks are a great start to being outside, observing nature and exploring your outdoor area. They can help children to feel comfortable in the outdoor environment, as well as being a great way to get from the nursery to the Forest School area.

Part of the magic of Forest School is getting ready to go out. Changing into outdoor clothes and preparing for the adventure makes the occasion special.

- Ask the children to find boots that are the same and match them into pairs. Talk about why welly boots are special – they can protect our feet from mud and water and keep the bottoms of our trousers dry.
- What noises can you make when walking in boots in different ways? Stomping, creeping, scraping, tapping, etc.
- On a wet day, paddling in puddles is great fun, and you will probably need to devote a session to this alone.
- On a windy day, let the children hold paper windmills or ribbons as you walk to see the force and direction of the wind.
- On a dry day, decorate welly boots using double-sided sticky tape on the outside (outer edge) of the welly boots, and collect leaves, grasses, flowers and feathers to make the wellies magnificent as you walk to your destination.
- Why not try putting some double-sided sticky tape on the bottom of welly boots and then walk through your Forest School area. What sticks to the boots? Scrape it off into a plant pot with some soil, leave it to germinate and see whether you picked up any seeds from the woodland floor.

Teaching tip

Initiating welly walks prior to starting Forest School sessions can ensure that parents understand the importance of the children being suitably dressed for whatever the weather. Pinpoint which parents you need to approach or whether you need to supply clothing for the children in your care.

Bonus idea ★

You can also collect leaves, petals and other natural objects on double-sided tape affixed to cardboard, to make sticky bracelets or forest crowns.

IDEA 6

Rope bus

'We have got a bit of a trek to get to our Forest School area, including walking through a car park and going down a slope.'

This is a simple idea to keep children safe when going from the classroom to the Forest School setting, and building their confidence to explore the outdoor area can be achieved by using this resource.

Teaching tip

When we get to the Forest School area, I lead the children around the fire area and we lay the rope on the ground. This then becomes the safety circle that the children do not cross.

Keeping children safe and together is important when getting from one location to another. I like using a rope bus. The children hold on and it gives them a sense of security when walking in places where they would normally have to hold an adult's hand.

- Get a long rope and ask the children to hold on to the rope bus; spread them out so that they do not trip over each other. Make knots along the rope or tie ribbons at regular intervals if the children 'bunch up' too much.
- This is a good introductory activity when taking small children outside, allowing them to explore a new area together. On subsequent sessions, you could reintroduce the rope bus for children to take turns in leading the others to explore different areas.
- Have some shorter ropes available (minibuses), suitable for about five children, so that they can lead each other around to explore the Forest School area.
- Why not go on a rope bus safari? Before the session, arrange your pictures of wildlife or toys along a route. Try to put animals in correct habitat areas – for example, you could have a picture of a worm on the ground, a rabbit at the entrance to a hole in the ground or a bird on the branch of a tree. Lead the children on a bus trip and when they see an animal, stop the bus so that they can pretend to take photographs of the animal and identify what it is.

IDEA 7

Tree decorating

'We have a special tree at Forest School that the children say hello to and they give it a hug when we arrive. It is called Old Oaky and he looks after the camp when we are not there.'

Many outdoor educators use the term 'vitamin N' (nature) for helping to build a love of the environment as well as enhancing well-being and resilience. This can start at an early age by children having a connection with their favourite tree.

Encouraging children to have a special connection to their area is one of the first steps to environmental stewardship.

- The environment is very resilient and will bounce back after children have been in the area. We should allow children to pick flower petals and leaves to use in activities, climb trees, move sticks from one area of the site to another and dig in the mud. The small damage that they will do in the short term is by far outweighed by the damage that can be done if the children reach adulthood and have no connection with the natural world.
- Let the children decorate their favourite tree to show their love for their environment.
- Use mud mixed with water for finger painting or use coloured chalks and charcoal to mark-make on the trunk of the tree.
- Use clay or sticky mud to make tree faces or woodland animals on the tree trunks. Use leaves, acorns seeds and grasses to enhance the features or make ears and whiskers.
- Wrap the trunk of a tree or low-hanging branches in ribbons, strips of material and hairy string to make the tree extra special.

Taking it further

If you have your own private area rather than public woods, leave up artwork and items made at Forest School in the woods to let the children have ownership of their area. Do not leave litter outside (bin it and take it with you), but having a pallet mud kitchen left in your area will not hurt it.

IDEA 8

Books in the woods

'We would like to extend our literacy sessions outside by having story-time around the campfire.'

Stories around the fire during a Forest School session are a chance for children to rest and recoup their energy. Plus, if you choose relevant books, it can be a great introduction to the next activity.

Teaching tip

Look on your nursery bookshelves and find books that are relevant to activities that children experience at Forest School. Some Forest School favourites are *The Very Hungry Caterpillar*, *The Bad-Tempered Ladybird* and *The Tiny Seed* by Eric Carle, *A Beginner's Guide to Bear Spotting* by Michelle Robinson and *Little Owl's Egg* by Debi Gliori, but I am sure there are many others you can find!

Lying on a picnic blanket, looking up at the branches of a tree whilst listening to a story, is one of my earliest memories and may have developed my love of reading today.

- Make a book tepee by lashing together some long, straight poles of similar length at the top end and standing them up. Spread out the legs to make a cone shape, making sure you leave a gap for the door, and peg some material around it to form a tepee.
- Furnish it with cushions and place some books in it for children to have a quiet book area.
- Alternatively, make a bed awning from a hula hoop and netting material, and hang it from a tree to make an instant tent.
- You could make a book tree by hanging lots of pieces of string from branches of a tree, long enough to reach the floor. Tie books onto the strings by opening the book to the middle page and tying the string securely around the centre of the book and the spine. The books will dangle just off the floor, ready for children to look at.

Using tools

Part 2

IDEA 9

Introducing using tools with young children

'Although I learnt how to use a range of tools during my training, I still haven't used them with children, as it worries me that something could go wrong so I just miss out that whole side of Forest School.' Forest School Leader, Plymouth

Tools introduce a new range of safety skills, ultimately promoting independence and risk-management skills. Children discover that using the right equipment for a job can save them time and effort, which is transferable to the skills they will need as an adult in the workaday world.

Using tools will promote strength, stamina, dexterity and coordination skills, as well as helping the children to achieve tasks and succeed, building their self-esteem and feelings of self-worth.

- Check that the tools are sharp and in good condition.
- Explain to the children that the tools are sharp, and introduce safety rules and procedures for how to use each tool for the task in hand.
- It is also important that any task set is appropriate, safe and achievable for the level, skill base and ability of the child.
- Support children when they are using tools in a ratio of one adult to one child.
- Set up a delegated tools area to ensure other people use the area safe. In many situations, a rope safety circle (Idea 10) will suffice.
- Children need to be confident and comfortable outside with themselves, the people they are with and the environment they are in before they will become comfortable and confident using tools.

Teaching tip

Before using tools with children, become confident in your own abilities to use each tool safely and correctly. There are various courses that may help increase your confidence and competence, such as TCV (The Conservation Volunteers). Local wildlife trusts, the National Trust and community woodland groups often run volunteer weekends and are happy to support developing tool skills in exchange for volunteering.

IDEA 10

The rope safety circle

'I need to make sure that children are not going to wander into my tool area when I'm working with other children.' Early Years Practitioner

Introduce a rope safety circle during outdoor sessions so that children have a visual barrier to demarcate areas they must not enter unless invited. Practise the importance of not entering the circle with children before the introduction of tools or fire.

We learn that if the circle is on the ground we always walk around it and never through it. This is achieved through reinforcement by playing circle games that ensure that no one enters the circle.

- I have used a rope safety circle for many years and, with practice, children even as young as two are able to recognise that the safety circle is not to be entered unless the child is invited by the adult.
- When using the rope circle, go to the edge of the circle and invite the child to accompany you to the centre to use the tools or approach the fire.
- When the child has finished, accompany them back to the edge of the circle and invite the next one to join you.
- If you have lots of adults assisting, you may want more than one adult in the circle using tools with children. If this is the case, ensure that the circle is large enough for you all to work comfortably, and do not allow children to stray into other tool-use zones whilst in the circle.

Teaching tip

Introduce the rope safety circle early on in your sessions, long before you plan to use fire or tools. Play games around the circle, use it as a gathering point and praise children for not entering the circle until it becomes second nature to them. Ask adult helpers to also respect the safety circle and not enter it, so the children have safe behaviour to observe and mimic.

IDEA 11

Low-risk tools

'Which tools are safe to use with children?' Teacher, Aberdeen

Showing children how to use tools safely can enhance your Forest School sessions, turning them into memorable experiences and expanding the range of activities you can achieve.

There are a range of tools that can be used outside with children. A tool is seen as an object that will help you achieve a job. No tool is safe if used incorrectly, so teaching the children to use tools in the correct fashion and to follow safety rules is of utmost importance.

- Scissors are a cutting tool. Encourage children to hold the closed blades in the palm of their hand when walking with scissors or passing them to someone else.
- Show the children how to hold a leaf with one hand and keep fingers out of the way when snipping.
- Use the correct scissors for the job – for instance, children's scissors, suitable for cutting paper and leaves, will struggle to cut through stems and fabric.
- Use scissors for cutting holes and shapes in leaves for mud-stencil painting; cutting string for a wide variety of activities; snipping off leaf stems to make leaf crowns; and cutting material and ribbons for craft activities.
- Mallets are hammering tools, usually made of wood or rubber, and are suitable for leaf bashing; knocking sticks or tent pegs into the ground; directing a blade when splitting wood; and flattening objects.
- Show the children how to keep fingers out of the way of the mallet.

Teaching tip

Keep tools in a toolbox or bag (ideally lockable or with a padlock) in clear sight, with a safety rope (Idea 10) around it to remind children that they must not touch it. For low-risk tools, a knotted drawstring bag may suffice but, again, makes unsupervised access difficult for children. A great idea observed at one nursery school, for transporting the tools to the Forest School area, was a hard-shell suitcase on wheels with a combination lock.

IDEA 12

Whittling tools

'I have been advised to not use knives with small children, only potato peelers, as they are lower risk.' Early Years Forest School Leader

Prior to using knives with children, many Forest School leaders like to introduce using potato peelers to remove bark from sticks to make toasting sticks for marshmallows.

Potato peelers give children the chance to practise the action required for the motion of going away from the body, and they make a great introduction to using knives.

- Knives are cutting tools. When using knives with children, it is important to emphasise that knives are tools for doing a job, like chopping vegetables or whittling wood.
- Store knives in a safe container, preferably stored within a toolbox or bag. Ensure that children do not wear a glove on the hand that is holding the knife.
- Demonstrate to the children how to cut away from themselves, and never towards themselves.
- Do not allow children to sit and work on their knees. If a child has mobility problems, work astride a log or with a rubber car mat laid over the legs.
- When using knives with children, have the child standing with an adult behind them, out of the line of vision of the child and guiding their hands, until the child can achieve the correct motion and angle to whittle effectively.
- Knives can be used for whittling the end of sticks for marshmallow-toasting or for removing bark and wood from sticks for a variety of craft activities.

Teaching tip

Have tins or lockable boxes for small, sharp tools, which little hands will not be able to open easily. Store them in your tool bag or toolbox and surround this by a rope safety circle (Idea 10), or put it out of reach when unattended.

IDEA 13

Loppers and secateurs

'Children have difficulty using loppers as they don't have enough strength to push the handles together.'

Children do not have to use tools the same way an adult would use them, but they can still be effective resources.

Teaching tip

Loppers can be used for cutting sticks to make forest friends, picture frames, magic wands, walking sticks, looms, etc. Secateurs are perfect for snipping twigs for willow whips.

With some small adjustments, there is no reason that all tools can't be made accessible to all children.

- Loppers are a type of secateur with long handles. Bypass loppers are those where a blade and bill slide past each other like scissors, and are good for close, clean cuts on live branches up to about 3.5 cm in diameter. Dead wood tends to get stuck in the blades. Anvil loppers, where a blade chops against the anvil plate, are suitable for using on dead wood up to 5 cm in diameter.
- Before using loppers, talk about safety and keeping fingers and toes away from the blades.
- Place the loppers with one handle on the ground and hold one handle to open the blades. Place a stick in the blades so that it is parallel to the ground. Let the child press down on the uppermost handle to cut the stick.
- Secateurs are scissor-like tools, much smaller than loppers and also known as hand pruners, and are used by holding them in one hand. Like loppers, there are two main types of secateurs – bypass and anvil – and they are used for snipping twigs and pruning shoots. Left-handed secateurs are available.
- Demonstrate that these tools have sharp blades. Children must keep both hands on the secateurs' handles at all times. If they use them one-handed, there is a greater risk of them catching fingers.

Bonus idea ★

If you have lost the blade covers that came with the tools when new, keep the blades closed by using elastic bands to hold them together, for storage or for when the tools are not in use.

IDEA 14

Sawing tools

'I like using the saw. It shakes my arms and is smelly!' Visually impaired child when cutting pine, chosen for its pungent aroma

Using a saw is noisy, uses gross motor skills and can be used to cut branches into usable lengths and make tree cookies (Idea 49).

Tools can be used by children of all ages and abilities. Sometimes you need to think about how to make an activity accessible to all children in your care, but it can be done.

- Bow saws have a coarse-toothed, wide blade, held in tension by the rainbow-shaped frame. They are used for cutting wood and branches up to about 15 cm in diameter.
- Secure the wood in a small saw horse so it will not bounce or move when you are sawing. Use clamps to make it more secure. Keep your non-tool hand away from the blade at all times. When using a bow saw with children, I ask them to keep both hands on the bow saw handle.
- If cutting a small branch, pre-cut a small groove for each tree cookie to be cut, and the children then have a starting point. Hold the branch about a body-width distance from the blade.
- Make sure that the saw cut is opening rather than compressing when you are cutting; adjust the position of the wood accordingly.
- If you need intricate cutting, use a hacksaw (small version of a bow saw with an added handle and a fine blade). Do not wear a glove on the tool hand.
- Make sure that when the saw is not being used, the blade cover is replaced, and hang it up out of reach or replace it in a tool bag, rather than leaving it lying on the ground.
- Use saws to cut poles for den building, making tree cookies (Idea 49) and cutting wood to size.

Taking it further

Folding or retracting saws can be used by embedding the blade within the wood and making a few saw strokes. Then ask the child to hold the handle with both hands to pull back and forth, or put their hand on top of your hand whilst sawing so they feel the vibration movement of the saw.

IDEA 15

Drilling tools

'We often need to make holes in wood. What is the best method?'

Making holes in wood can extend projects at Forest School, such as making holes for tree cookies (see Idea 49), making wheels for vehicles and adding twigs to sticks for arms and legs for small-people play.

There are a variety of hole-making tools that you can use at Forest School.

- Hand drills amplify the circular movement of the turning crank to turn the bit and drill a hole. They hold drill bits from 1 mm to 9 mm. Clamp the wood you are drilling or ask someone else to hold it securely. Hold the drill vertically and turn it in a clockwise direction. I often find that two children can use this tool very efficiently together.
- A brace and bit are used to make larger holes or to work with larger pieces of wood. I have found these to be the most difficult drilling tool for younger children to use.
- A palm drill is a drill bit mounted and secured into a handle, small and light. It is a useful tool when drilling a small number of holes. They are relatively cheap to buy and light to carry. Use a palm drill safely by positioning the wood to be drilled either on the ground or on a firm surface. Do not drill into your hand or leg. Press down and twist.
- Use battery-powered electric drills by making sure that the wood to be drilled is held securely and gently pressed whilst pressing the 'on' button. To remove the drill bit from wood, change the switch to reverse mode.
- All of these drilling tools can be used for any activity that requires holes being made in wood, such as tree cookies (Idea 49), beads and inserting dowelling axels into cookie wheels to make vehicles.

Taking it further

It is possible to make your own palm drill by fixing a drill bit into a wooden handle, or alternatively make your own handle by using hand-mouldable plastic (also known as polymorph). I have used this to make customised handles for children who need adaptable tools, to make an activity more accessible for them.

Part 3

Fire

IDEA 16

Getting ready for fire

'What do we need to prepare to have a fire at Forest School?' Early Years Foundation Stage (EYFS) Practitioner

Make sessions memorable at Forest School by introducing a fire. It can be used to make warm drinks, cook food and give warmth on a cold day, as well as being a good focal point to bring the group together to talk and reflect.

Teaching tip

When you have a fire, always keep a bucket of water next to it to douse the flames if necessary. This bucket can also be used to plunge a hand or limb in if anyone burns themselves. An old hand towel soaked in the bucket can also be used as a fire blanket. Keep a pair of welding gloves to hand, so you can remove kettles and pans from the fire easily without burning yourself.

There are several factors you need to take into consideration to keep yourself, the children in your care and your Forest School area safe when using fire in your sessions.

- Check that your nursery insurance allows for having a fire on your premises.
- If you are in woodlands owned by another party, check that you are allowed to have a fire.
- Find an area with a clear space of at least 2 m by 2 m.
- Clear the ground of any leaf litter so that you are down to bare earth. If the ground is dry, soak the ground with water first. If you are building a permanent fire area, putting some hard core, fire bricks or sand underneath compacted soil will make your area safer.
- Make sure you are not under any low-hanging tree branches and away from visible tree roots and bushes.
- Mark out your area and ensure that seating (small logs, benches or sit mats) are at least 1.5 m away from the fire. Place a rope (I use a white one for ease of visibility) on the ground just inside the seating circle, and make sure that the children understand that they are not to enter this area at any time unless accompanied by an adult (Idea 10). Train children how to behave in the fire area, how to approach the fire and how to leave it, and never leave the fire unattended by an adult.

- Make sure that your fire area is four or more metres away from any shelters or activity areas.
- Use logs, rocks or fire bricks to outline the fire hearth. Fix logs in place with pegs to ensure that they do not roll.
- Do not build a fire in a coniferous area or on peat soil as fire can smoulder and travel under the ground. Do not light a fire in very dry or windy conditions.
- If you want to use a temporary fire area, fire bowls are available from supermarkets and camping shops. You can also use low barbecues and metal trays as alternatives.
- Make sure that long hair is tied back and that fleeces, man-made fibres and loose clothing are not worn around the fire.
- Always have sufficient water ready to douse the fire, and make sure it is completely out and all evidence removed before you leave the area. Scatter leaves over the area afterwards to make it as natural as possible.
- Always keep a first aid kit to hand.

> **Bonus idea**
>
> A storm kettle or Kelly Kettle™ (available online or from some camping shops) is a real bonus for outdoor sessions, and gives you the ability to build a small fire to have hot drinks, even when you are not having a large fire in your session.

IDEA 17

How to light a fire

'Initially getting a fire going was difficult but worth practising, because it really enhances our sessions. The children find watching the flames mesmerizing.' Forest School leader

Fire lighting is a skill that needs practising before you can use it in your sessions.

Preparation is the key to success. Children can be involved in finding and sorting the different materials that you need to accomplish the task.

- Before you start, ensure you have the following: matches or a fire strike; plenty of tinder to start the fire – dried grass, nettle stalks, pine needles, gorse, birch bark, etc.; about five or six larger sticks, thicker than your thumb, to make a platform for your fire; and kindling and fuel bundles – very thin twigs, twigs the thickness of a pencil lead, twigs the thickness of a pencil, twigs the thickness of your finger and then larger sticks to keep your fire going.
- Always have plenty of water to hand.
- Lay the platform and use the tinder to make a base for the fire.
- Use some small kindling to build a pyramid around the tinder.
- Light the match or fire strike close to the kindling by striking it away from your body. Keep feeding your fire with fuel once it is lit.
- Once the fire is lit, do not leave it unattended.
- When you want to put the fire out, stop feeding it fuel and allow the fire to go to a smoulder. Once this has happened, sprinkle water over the fire to stop the smoulder.
- When the fire is out and cold, pick up the remains and dispose of them responsibly if you are not using your regular fire area. Nobody should be able to see that you have lit a fire there.

Teaching tip

If the fire does not catch, try blowing on it gently or wafting it to introduce more oxygen to help reignite it.

Bonus idea ★

Carry a pre-prepared tinder bundle in a zip top bag so that you know your tinder is dry and you can make fire no matter what! You can add in anything that is dry, such as cotton wool, shredded tissues, old bus tickets and wood shavings.

IDEA 18

Making charcoal in a tin

'When you sniff the tin, it smells really yuck – not like it smelt when we put the sticks in!'

A science experiment in a tin! This demonstrates changing states and that heat can help us to make resources for Forest School.

Children can experiment with burning to find out how we can make our own resources for drawing.

- The resources you will need are a tin with a close-fitting lid (a large Golden Syrup™ tin works well), secateurs, fresh twigs the diameter of a drinking straw (hazel, birch and willow work well) and a fire.
- Make a hole in the lid of the tin with a screwdriver or a hammer and nail.
- Support the children to use the secateurs (see Idea 13) to cut a couple of twigs, each about the length of their index finger, and pop them in the tin.
- Make sure that the fire is not roaring, but is a low fire with lots of embers. Push the lid on firmly and place it on the fire, carefully using two stout sticks or some welding gloves.
- You will observe a white smoke and steam coming out of the hole. When the smoke turns dark, carefully remove the tin from the fire, cover the hole with a lump of mud and allow it to cool.
- Gather the group close when you open the tin so that they get a whiff of the pungent charcoal smell when the tin is opened. They will be able to observe a dark tar residue inside the tin; the sticks will have turned into charcoal. They can now be used for other activities (see Ideas 20 and 49 for things to do with this free resource).
- If your tin is full of ash rather than charcoal sticks, you have left it on the fire too long.

Teaching tip

Use the charcoal you have made to draw a postcard or picture of children's favourite activity at Forest School. You can use this as a reflective exercise.

Involving parents

How about inviting parents to join a session? Pre-prepare the invitations by printing information on one side of some card and let the children draw their favourite things about learning outside on the other with charcoal. 'Fix' the charcoal with hairspray or artist's pastel fixative spray.

IDEA 19

Making firelighters

'The firelighters we made last time made the fire really big so we could toast our marshmallows.'

Getting started with a campfire is simplified by having this resource made by the children to get the fire going.

Making our own resources is a great activity to involve children in understanding the need for preparation, as well as the need for gathering dry materials to get the fire going well.

- Every child will need an individual egg holder, torn from a cardboard egg box.
- Look around your area and gather dry resources such as dried grass, thistledown, very thin, dry twigs and bark.
- You can also include some shredded paper and tumble dryer lint. Use a mixture of materials to make a fluffy nest in the cup.
- Stand an empty, clean baked beans can in a pot of very hot water and melt some candle stubs or broken crayons in it. Stir with a stick until melted.
- Carefully dribble melted wax into each egg cup nest and leave to harden. This will hold the materials in place as well as being flammable.
- Store the finished firelighters in a waterproof box until needed.
- To light a fire using these firelighters, place the egg cup on a little raft of stout sticks to lift it off the ground and give it some air flow. Using a match, light the cardboard edge of the egg holder and build a tepee of thin twigs around it.
- This is a particularly useful resource to have on a damp day, as the wax burns hot and lasts for about five minutes, which is much longer than just dry tinder, giving the sticks around it time to dry and catch.

Teaching tip

Only use egg boxes in school and nursery settings if they look clean and do not have spillages from cracked eggs visible on them. If you want to be extra vigilant (especially if there are egg allergies in your setting), you may want to microwave the box for a minute to sterilise it.

Involving parents

Ask parents for some of the ingredients. Lots of parents will happily donate egg boxes, old candles and broken crayons, and who would ever have a use for their tumble dryer lint?

IDEA 20

Fire words mobile

'We used this activity in our nursery when we were exploring Holi, the Hindu festival that takes place at the start of spring.'

Sitting around the fire is a perfect time to talk. This collective making of a fire words mobile is a great activity for extending vocabulary, using adjectives, and reflecting and exploring cultures and traditions.

Explore the features and properties of fire to encourage children's imagination and make a visual reminder of the fire to take back to the classroom.

- When sitting around the fire with children, talk about what they can see, what they can smell and what they feel.
- Ask each child to think about two words describing the fire. Maybe they will choose the colours, the movement, the sounds, the smells or the heat.
- On brightly coloured card (orange, red and yellow) cut out flame shapes and allow the children to decorate them with charcoal and coloured pens.
- Write the adjectives describing the fire suggested by the children onto the flame shapes. Use both sides of the card.
- Hole-punch the card, both top and bottom, and thread it on some string, linking it with everybody else's words to make a fire word mobile. Tie some twigs to the bottom of the mobile to represent the wood on the fire.
- Hang the finished mobile from a tree, well away from the fire.

Taking it further

If you laminate the words, the mobile can be left outside in your Forest School area.

Bonus idea ★

Explore the Hindu festival of Holi, which celebrates when good triumphed over evil. Last year's rubbish is burned in a bonfire so that people can start afresh. You can use this idea to throw 'bad' thoughts and feelings away. Children say the things that make them sad, worried or angry to a piece of paper, then screw it up and pop it into a bowl. You then throw all the paper into the fire.

IDEA 21

Campfire cookery

'I worry about cleanliness and food poisoning when cooking over the fire.' Nursery Manager, Essex

Fire is a great resource for the outdoor classroom to experiment with food preparation and cooking.

When preparing and cooking food outside, observe good food hygiene standards, similar to those you would use within the classroom to ensure food safety.

- Keep hands clean when cooking and handling food. Use antiseptic wipes or soap and water or use running water. Dry hands well, using paper towels. Clean hands before and after handling food, and after going to the toilet, sneezing, coughing or blowing your nose.
- Set up a handwashing station with bottles of water, soap and handtowels. A solar shower is great for this as it can be hung from a branch and turned on for running water.
- Cooking destroys bacteria that can cause food poisoning. Ensure food is thoroughly cooked through. Do not cook any meat on the bone and always split meat open and ensure it is cooked inside as well as outside before eating.
- Keep cooked foods and raw foods separate from each other and be careful to avoid cross-contamination.
- Ensure that all cooking pots, pans and utensils are clean before you use them. You can make sure that things do not get dirty or contaminated when outside before using them to cook by covering them with cling film or putting them into a sealed bag.

Teaching tip

Easy things to cook that do not require much preparation include toasted brioche, croissants or crumpets; packet Frankfurters; marshmallows cooked on a stick; packet cake mixes cooked in a scooped-out orange shell; and finally, hot chocolate.

- If you are cooking using a stick – for example, toasting marshmallows or bannocks (Idea 22) – use a green stick and remove the bark with a potato peeler.
- Store food in cool boxes. Keep food covered wherever possible to help prevent bacteria as well as birds, insects and hungry squirrels from stealing your food.
- Reduce handling if possible – for instance, mix ingredients in a zip top bag or using tongs.
- When you have cooked food, it should be eaten as soon as possible. Do not reheat it.
- Keep cuts and sores covered with a waterproof dressing. If it's on the hand, also wear disposable gloves to give added protection, but remember to wash the gloves as if they were hands.
- Wash hands before eating.

> **Bonus idea** ★
>
> If the children are interested, divide any mixture that requires kneading into several ziplock bags. Encourage the children to knead through the bag (no messy fingers) to develop their fine motor skills.

IDEA 22

Bannock

'We have cooked marshmallows over the fire but would like to try some more things that are simple to prepare.'

Cooking over the fire is great fun, and children enjoy having the chance to experiment with lots of different foods. A simple food that is easy to prepare and keep clean in the outdoor environment is bannock, which is a Scottish scone bread recipe.

Taking it further

Experiment with the basic recipe by adding in sultanas, sugar and cinnamon at the kneading stage or, for a savoury taste, try herbs and grated cheese.

Here's a recipe to make a basic bannock, which can be adapted to suit the tastes and dietary needs of your group.

- Choose some fresh, long sticks (hazel works well), at least the length of an adult arm and the thickness of your little finger. Using potato peelers or whittling knives, remove the bark at one end so you have clean wood. Let each child have one stick.
- Using zip top plastic bags (one between two children), add in the following ingredients: one cup of flour, one level teaspoon of baking powder, one tablespoon of cooking oil and one cup of warm water.
- Close the bag, exclude as much air as possible and seal it.
- Knead the bag with your hands until all of the ingredients are mixed up into a soft ball of dough. Let the children share this task.
- When the dough has formed, put a clean green stick into the bag and, using half the dough, form a 'sausage' shape of dough onto the end of the stick.
- Hold the stick over the campfire hot coals – not flames – turning frequently for about ten minutes until it is golden brown.
- When it has cooled to warm, you can eat it as it is or you can spread on some jam or honey, or even pesto and cream cheese.

IDEA 23

Chapattis

'We don't have much time to prepare food during our Forest School sessions but would like to have something prepared beforehand that we can take with us to cook on the fire. As a healthy eating nursery, we discourage recipes with lots of sugar.' Nursery Manager, Milton Keynes

A recipe that is easy to prepare and can be used to explore foods from different cultures.

There are many things that can be prepared in advance. This is a favourite recipe of mine on a cold day, as an accompaniment to a flask of hot soup.

- Whilst still in the classroom, put 250 g of plain flour into a bowl. Gradually stir in 80 ml of warm water with a knife until a ball of dough is formed. Add more flour if it gets sticky. Knead the dough on a floured plate for five minutes until elastic. Cover the dough and leave for an hour. Pop it into a clean, food-safe container with a lid and take it with you to your Forest School site.
- Just prior to cooking, wash your hands and knead the dough again for a couple of minutes. Divide the dough into golf-ball-sized balls, roll in flour and flatten into a thin round.
- Cook the chapatti in a lightly oiled frying pan over the fire (hot embers rather than flames) for about 30 seconds on each side. Put the chapatti onto a clean tea towel and press to swell it up, or put it on a griddle on the fire.

Teaching tip

Eat the chapatti hot as it is or it is lovely served as an accompaniment to other foods, such as dahl, soup or with a bit of butter. Why not try wrapping it around a hotdog previously warmed on a stick?

IDEA 24

Foil parcels

'We grow lots of different vegetables in our nursery garden. We would like to use these at Forest School for cooking over the fire.'
Early Years Manager, Plymouth

There are lots of recipes involving vegetables that are easy to cook on a campfire.

This recipe is very flexible and can be tailored to individual tastes and the availability of the vegetables you have to hand.

- Vegetables can be prepared in advance or cut up on site. Why not have the vegetables pre-chopped into similar-sized pieces in zip top bags? Then the children can select the ones that they like to construct their parcels.
- Before you start cooking, make sure that your hands and equipment are clean.
- Place one square of foil on top of another one and brush the top one with oil. You can put the foil into a small bowl to make it easier to fill.
- Place in the vegetables and add salt, pepper and maybe a few herbs if you want to, along with a tablespoon of water.
- Wrap the inner foil and seal by scrunching up the edges. Reinforce your parcel by wrapping the second square of foil around it. Place it in the embers of the fire.
- Cook for 15 to 30 minutes, depending on the contents of your parcel, until the vegetables are cooked.
- Try out different combinations in your parcel – why not try a root vegetable parcel? Put in some (or all) of the following vegetables: potato, swede, parsnip, onion, carrot and sweet potato. Or how about a Mediterranean vegetable parcel, with a mixture of red, yellow and green peppers, cherry tomatoes, onions, courgettes and mushrooms?

Teaching Tip

This method is great for sweet dishes too. Why not try a hot fruit parcel of apple, pear, plum and blackberries? This is lovely served by itself or with some cream.

Bonus idea ★

Large potatoes or whole individual sweet potatoes are particularly delicious when wrapped in foil and cooked in the embers of the fire for up to an hour, depending on size, and served with some butter.

IDEA 25

Nettle soup

'There is an area of stinging nettles in our Forest School site, which the children keep away from. We are not sure what to do with them.'

The children will be fascinated by this introduction to the world of foraging and using resources they have found in your area.

Stinging nettles can be reduced in your area by frequent strimming or cutting back with shears, but they do make a good resource too. Tea can be made by popping the top couple of leaves from a nettle into boiling water, leaving them to brew for a few minutes and then straining for a healthy drink. And then there is soup...

- Collect nettle tops (just the first four to six leaves) in your carrier bag using the scissors to cut them. Remember to wear gloves and long sleeves or you could get stung. Wash the nettles and remove the thickest stalks.
- Chop up an onion and cook it in a pan with a little oil until soft. Add in a large diced potato and some finely chopped celery and cook for five minutes over the fire. Finely chop a garlic clove and add it to the pot.
- Put the nettle leaves into the pot and cook for a few minutes until wilted, then add in some boiling water to cover all the ingredients.
- Crumble in vegetable stock cubes and bring to the boil for about 20 minutes.
- Remove from the fire and allow to cool.
- Using a metal sieve, strain the liquid into a bowl or another pot, then push the mixture through the sieve using the back of a spoon to purée it.
- Stir in some milk or cream and bring it back to the boil, stirring frequently, and then serve.

Teaching tip

Using natural resources in recipes is a good introduction to foraging with children and a great skill, which will last them a lifetime. Make sure that they know never to try anything outside unless you have given it to them.

Bonus idea ★

Nettles also make lovely crisps by frying individual nettle leaves in oil for 30 seconds until crisp. Remove from the oil with a slotted spoon and drain on some kitchen paper. Sprinkle lightly with salt to taste and serve.

IDEA 26

Making popcorn

'Pop, pop, pop. That's the best snack!' Three-year-old child, Callington, Cornwall

Making popcorn over the fire is one of those magical experiences that assault the senses – you see it, hear it, touch it, smell it and then you taste it. Science in action!

Often children have experienced eating packaged popcorn with their families, but making it over the campfire will extend their knowledge of what they eat and how it is made.

Teaching tip

You will need a fire that has burnt down to hot embers for the best results.

Method 1:

- Get two metal sieves the same size. Lash one onto a sturdy stick with string or wire. The other sieve needs to be attached to the first sieve with either wire or keyring jump rings, via the metal bits you use to stand them on a saucepan, to form a dome.
- Place a handful of un-popped corn kernels (available from supermarkets and health food shops) inside.
- Gently shake the sieves over hot embers and, after a few minutes, you will see the kernels pop into white popcorn. Cool slightly and tip into a bowl to share.
- Although delicious, this method of cooking sometimes leaves a smoky taste.

Method 2:

- Put two tablespoons of cooking oil into a heavy-bottomed pan with a close fitting lid.
- Place it over the embers of the fire to heat, shaking the pan occasionally. (Wear welders gloves, available from DIY stores, to do this.)
- You will hear lots of popping. Remove from the fire and open the lid carefully. Spoon out the popcorn and share.

Bonus idea ★

If you want to flavour the popcorn, try dissolving a couple of teaspoons of salt with some malt vinegar in a spray bottle and spray it on warm popcorn for a salt and vinegar flavour. Sweet popcorn can be made by melting some butter and honey or demerara sugar together and drizzling over the popcorn. Make sure it cools sufficiently before serving.

IDEA 27

Roasting sweet chestnuts

'We have a sweet chestnut tree on our school grounds. The children like collecting the prickly cases, which they call baby hedgehogs and they cuddle with the greatest of care.'

If you are lucky enough to have a sweet chestnut tree on your grounds, the children will enjoy foraging their own food to try. Otherwise, you could bring some onto the site and maybe plant a few of the nuts to see if you can grow a tree for future generations of children.

Sweet chestnut trees were introduced to the UK by the Romans, who used them to make flour. The sweet chestnut cases are prickly, with fine, long spikes. If you have access to a sweet chestnut tree, collect the nuts from late autumn onwards.

- Wear thick gloves to save fingers from being prickled and remove the nuts from their cases. There are usually three or four nuts in each case.
- Soak the nuts for 30 minutes in a bowl of water, then make a cross with a knife on the flat side of the shell. Do not cut too deeply – you want to cut through the shell but not the meat underneath. Cutting the chestnuts will prevent them from exploding, and makes them easier to peel when cooked.
- Place the nuts in a pan over the fire and roast for about 20 to 30 minutes, until the shell has curled open or you can see steam and hear them hissing.
- Wait for them to cool slightly then peel the shell off and eat.
- Please check for allergies before giving to your children.

Including parents

This makes a lovely activity for family celebration days and provides a really traditional vegan Christmas snack for everyone to try.

Taking it further

If you do not eat them all, chop them and add them to either fresh or packet cake mix and cook it in the empty shell of an orange in the embers of the fire. Alternatively, mix them into soups and stews for extra taste.

IDEA 28

Cooking with apples

'We have our Forest School sessions in a local orchard and during the autumn there is an abundance of fruit to use.' Head Teacher, Devon

There are lots of lovely recipes you can cook using orchard fruits. Here are a few of my favourite ones.

Involving parents

This makes a lovely activity for harvest festival; invite families to come and share the autumn bounty.

What can be fresher than fruit picked straight from the tree? When preparing apples, give them a wash in some water to remove any dirt, dust or spray residue, and cut them on a hard surface such as a plate or a chopping board.

Toffee apple slices

- Cut an apple into quarters or sixths, depending on the size of the apples. Place the pieces onto a sharp stick.
- Dip the apple slices into a container of sugar and cinnamon mixed together and toast over the fire, turning frequently. Cool before eating.

Orchard parcels

- These are great when you have a variety of different fruits available, such as apples, pears and plums. You can also add in some blackberries if available.
- Chop up the fruit into bite-sized chunks, remove all stones and pips and place onto a square of kitchen foil. If the fruit varieties you have access to tend to be tart, drizzle some runny honey or maple syrup over the fruit chunks and gather the edges of the foil together to make a parcel.
- Turn the parcel over several times to allow the honey to cover all the fruit and place in the embers of the fire.
- Cook for ten to 15 minutes, then remove from the fire. When sufficiently cooked, eat directly from the foil with a fork or carefully tip into an ice cream cornet to serve.

Stuffed apples

- To make stuffed apples, core the apple and place onto a foil square.
- In a separate container, mix together sultanas, brown sugar and cinnamon and spoon into the hole left by the removed apple core.
- Wrap the apple into a parcel by gathering the foil at the top. Place on the embers of the fire and cook for ten to 15 minutes until the flesh of the apple is soft.
- Remove from the fire and allow to sufficiently cool before eating. Serve with a dollop of plain yoghurt, or cream if you are feeling particularly naughty.

Easy apple juice

- Cut up the apples into small pieces. There is no need to remove the peel.
- Put the cut apple into a large saucepan and cover with water.
- Put the pan onto the embers of the fire and bring it to a simmer. Take the pan off the fire every now and then and mash the apple using a potato masher until the apple flesh is broken down.
- Leave to cool until it is just warm, then strain into a clean container using a fine mesh sieve.
- Stir in sugar to taste, especially if the apples are tart.

> **Bonus idea** ★
>
> Explore the properties of an apple with the children by letting them hold one and feel the firm, smooth skin. Ask them to smell it. Can they see the bottom of the apple, which was the centre of the flower? Can they see where it was attached to the tree? Cut through the middle with a knife and open the apple to reveal the star inside. Why not try planting some of the seeds to grow a new apple tree?

IDEA 29

Hot bananas

'Whenever Forest School is mentioned in our house, my husband shouts out "Hot bananas!". We had to make them on the barbecue this summer.' Parent of Forest School Child

With a little assistance, the children can customise their own bananas — a lovely warm snack for a cold day outside.

This is a firm favourite for Forest School feasts and is lovely for family celebration days, as everyone can make their own to their individual tastes.

- Make sure that each child has clean hands and give them each a square of foil.
- Put a banana in the centre with the stalk pointing upwards. Carefully cut through the skin of the banana lengthways.
- Slice through the flesh of the banana with a sharp knife, but be careful not to cut through the skin on the bottom. Push chocolate buttons (both milk chocolate and white chocolate work well) into the slot. Add in some mini marshmallows if you want.
- Scrunch the foil around the banana to make a parcel. Carefully put it in the hot embers of the fire, using tongs, and cook until the banana flesh is hot and soft and the chocolate has melted.
- Remove from the fire and leave to cool down a bit until they are ready to eat. You can either split the skin further and eat it direct from the foil package (wrap in a paper towel first to prevent soot transference onto hands and clothing) or you can scoop the flesh into a bowl to eat it with a spoon.
- If you do not want to use chocolate and marshmallows because of the sugar content, the bananas are still lovely when cooked without these additions and served with a dollop of plain yoghurt.

Taking it further

We have done this activity as a hot snack with a group of parents (children were not present), as we were preparing a very overgrown site to be a Forest School area for a school. We finished off the bananas with a teaspoon of rum sprinkled over the banana flesh for a more adult taste.

Trees and leaves

Part 4

IDEA 30

Leaf sewing

'We have a ten-minute walk to our Forest School area. I like to find activities to do on the way.' Forest School Leader

Children love collecting things on walks, and leaf sewing works really well for small children as a travelling activity to get you from one point to another, especially on a damp autumn day, as the leaves tend to be a bit more pliable and less crumbly.

Threading the leaves is a good activity for developing finger muscles ready for pencil control at a later stage.

- Each child will need a pipe cleaner (the long ones work best and can usually be found in craft shops) and a large bead.
- Prepare the pipe cleaner by threading the bead onto the end and folding over the end to stop it coming off.
- As you walk through the woods, thread leaves onto the pipe cleaner by pushing leaves onto the end of the wire and gently pushing them down to where the bead is stopping them from falling off the end.
- Make a collection of colourful autumn leaves. Hang them individually or as a group on a piece of cord strung between two trees for display.

Taking it further

Why not decorate the leaves with patterns or nature-inspired pictures using gold and silver pens or fine-liner permanent pens? This encourages mark-making for pre-writers. A lovely reflective activity is to write hopes and wishes on them as you thread them on the pipe cleaner. I have used this with children moving up to primary school and also with bereaved children when involved in a counselling project to help them to process their loss.

Bonus idea ★

This can also be extended into a group activity by selecting leaves and decorating them, or writing wishes or reflections on leaves, and pegging them onto a string stretched between trees for display.

IDEA 31

Hessian pictures

'I made my mummy a present for her birthday. Look at the feathers and the flowers. I poked them with a stick. She is a very lucky mummy.'

A natural piece of artwork that you can make and take home to share with families is a great way to show parents what their child is creating at Forest School. It is also a great talking point, as children can retell the process they had to go through to achieve the piece.

This activity is a great introduction for whittling sticks to make children's own tools and resources.

- Select a stick about the length of a pencil and, using a knife or a potato peeler, carefully whittle the stick to a sharp point
- Give each participant a piece of hessian, about 20 cm by 20 cm, or smaller if you want to mount them onto cards. Hessian is a strong, coarse fabric made from hemp or jute and used for making sacks or by upholsterers. It has a loose weave and is easily available from material shops and craft shops.
- Gather a range of natural materials, such as grasses, flowers with stalks, reeds, feathers, lichens, leaves and twigs, and, using the pointed stick, gently ease the hessian fibres apart to make a hole. Carefully poke the natural materials through the hessian.
- Colourful ribbon can also be easily poked through the holes to make an effective running stitch or outline.
- Build up the hessian hanging and then display it by attaching it to a straight stick with staples or glue, or sewing a loop to hold it on the stick.

Taking it further

When cutting the hessian, make it slightly smaller than A5. When completed, stick it onto an A4 piece of card folded in half to make a greeting card, and use it for Mother's, Father's or Grandparent's Day greetings cards.

IDEA 32

Colour postcards

'This is like magic. I never knew you could paint with flowers.' Early Years Student, Duchy College, Cornwall

This is not only a very visual activity but it also provides lovely aromas to stimulate children's sense of smell. This is also a good way to explore the wide range of colours available in the natural world.

Nature provides us with a great array of natural resources, with lots of colours, shades and hues, all of which are exciting to explore with children.

- Give each child a plain postcard. Alternatively, you could use white card instead.
- Go on a walk around your Forest School area to see what colours you can see. Find some grass, rip it several times and rub the raw edges on the card. This will give you a green colour. This also works well with fresh leaves. Do not use evergreen leaves, as they do not give good results.
- Have a look at the flowers you have in your area. Dandelions, buttercups and the centre of daisies will give you the colour yellow. Pink campion flowers will initially mark-make in pink but, when exposed to the air, will rapidly turn to a blue hue.
- Dandelion stalks will give brown. Blackberries give a purple colour.
- You can also draw with mud on your fingers or a twig and charcoal from previous fires.
- Experiment and find out which natural colours you can make using what you can find in your area.
- Why not draw pictures of the Forest School area or portraits of each other?
- It is important to be aware of what plant life is in your outdoor area and avoid poisonous plants or irritants.

Involving parents

You can help the children to write a message to their parents on the back of the postcards. Why not include a trip to the nearest postbox and post the cards home? These make a lovely way of inviting families to join you for celebration sessions at Forest School.

IDEA 33

Autumn leaf spiral mobile

'We love exploring the changes and colours of autumn at Forest School. The children initiated a great game of trying to catch the leaves as they fell from the trees every time the wind blew.'
Preschool Practitioner, Kent

Watching leaves swirl down from the trees in a light autumn breeze can be a magical experience for children. This activity recreates this experience so it can be enjoyed again and again.

Taking children outside on a regular basis throughout the year gives them an opportunity to experience the changes in the seasons. Autumn brings a cornucopia of colours and crunchy fallen leaves. Nothing beats jumping in a pile of leaves or transporting armfuls of leaf litter from one place to another, but you can also take advantage of a ready supply of free resources to use in craft and seasonal activities.

- Give each child a paper plate or a circle of cardboard and help them in cutting a spiral shape.
- Using one side of a hole punch, make a hole at one end of the spiral.
- Looking around your Forest School area, collect as many different-coloured and different-shaped leaves as you can. Look for yellows, reds and oranges as well as browns and greens.
- Glue the autumnal leaves to the card all the way along the spiral. You can use both sides.
- Thread some string through the hole and hang the spiral up.
- When it spins and moves in the breeze, it will look like the leaves are tumbling down from the trees.

Teaching tip

Show the children how to draw a snail shell onto the paper plate to give them a cutting guide to making the spiral.

Bonus idea ★

Visit your local DIY shop and pick up free paint colour charts. Choose some with typically autumnal colours. Give them to the children and see if they can find the matching colours in the Forest School area.

IDEA 34

Autumn leaf wreath

'It's autumn. The leaves fall off the trees so I can collect them. Thank you tree!' Three-year-old child (said when hugging a tree), Cornwall

Make wreaths to decorate your classroom and show off the beauty of the autumnal colours found outside the classroom.

Autumn is a magical time when nature provides us with lots of free resources whilst preparing itself for winter. Making a wreath to celebrate the colours of autumn is a lovely activity and looks wonderful back in the classroom.

- Cut some long willow shoots (about six to ten per wreath) with some secateurs (see Idea 13) and gently bend them to form a circle. Carefully twist the sticks around each other and secure them using string or ribbon.
- Decorate your wreath by weaving in autumnal leaves and flowers or, in winter, holly and ivy. To make the wreath extra special, attach a range of natural resources such as seed cases, acorns, conkers, pine cones, etc. You can use cotton or string, but if you want a more robust wreath, you could also use floristry wire or a glue gun to do this.
- A simpler version, so that every child can have their own wreath, is to use paper plates with the centre cut out.
- Collect a range of leaves of different colours, shapes, sizes, etc., and arrange them on the cardboard template. You may want to create a spectrum of leaf colours or a wreath of as many different shapes or sizes as you can find. When you are happy with your arrangement, stick the leaves onto the cardboard ring.
- Use double-sided tape (the sort used to stick down carpets works the best) or glue, and attach a ribbon or string to the top of the wreath to hang it up.

> **Bonus idea** ★
>
> You can reuse the willow wreath by removing any dead vegetation and adding in new leaves, so your decorations change according to the season. For instance, a spring wreath could have spring flowers and catkins, whereas a Christmas wreath could have holly, ivy, bells and pine cones.

IDEA 35

Leaf fishing

'We have been exploring magnets and learning new vocabulary such as "attract", "repel" and "magnet". The children are fascinated by this new concept and enjoy experimenting and making predictions with the magnet collection.'

Take classroom learning outside and use natural resources along with magnets as a new way to learn.

Using scientific equipment outside the classroom can develop children's curiosity and help them understand that science can happen anywhere.

- Collect a range of leaves and put a paper clip on each one. Make a 'pond' by placing a string circle on the ground. Put the leaves with paper clips into the string circle.
- Find a stick about the length of your forearm and tie on a piece of string (the length of your arm) with a magnet on the end to make a fishing rod. Go fishing in your leaf pool.

Here are some examples of the way you can use this game, but it is flexible to fit in with anything you are learning about with the children.

- Leaf numbers: write numbers on the leaves, add together your catch and the highest score wins.
- Leaf words: write sounds or letters on the leaves, and fish to make words. Children could find the initial letter of their name or practise whole-word recognition using their names. They could take it in turns to fish for a name, and the person written on the leaf can decide on the next activity or instigate the next game.
- Story sequencing: drawing pictures on the leaves and telling a story in the order that the leaves are fished can be a very funny activity for children to participate in.

Teaching tip

The shorter the string, the easier it is to control the fishing rod to 'catch' a leaf fish. If a child is struggling to catch anything, shorten their string.

IDEA 36

Leaf masks for forest superheroes

'When I am a man, I am going to be a superhero. I'm going to save the world and look after baby animals.' Dan, aged four

Superhero play is something that engages children's imaginations when role-playing and allows them to explore their interests. This is supported in the EYFS, which highlights the idea that effective learning starts with child-led play, and practitioners must reflect the different ways that children learn.

This activity is great when covering a superhero topic or just because everybody needs to be a superhero once in a while.

- Make card-template eye masks. Hole-punch and reinforce the holes, ready for the string or elastic. Each child needs a blank eye mask.
- Collect natural materials such as leaves, petals and grasses, and glue or stick onto the mask.
- Wait until the mask is dry and then add elastic or string ties to tie the mask to the child's face.
- Ask the children to think about their superhero superpowers and special talents.
- Extend children's imaginative play by providing a range of large, square scarves to make superhero cloaks. You can pick up large scarves very cheaply in charity shops and jumble sales.

Taking it further

Weapon play can offer children the opportunity to explore a range of ideas and emotions in a safe environment and learn how to deal with conflict in an emotionally safe way. If weapons are not an issue at your setting, think about helping children to make stick swords and shields, or even basic bows and arrows to extend their play.

IDEA 37

Woodland magic

'My favourite story is *Room on the Broom*. I made a broomstick and made magic in the woods.'

Integrate favourite classroom books and tales into your Forest School sessions by using natural resources to make props to complement the stories.

Basing a session around the interests of the children can lead to deep-level learning experiences and help them engage fully in the process.

- To make a broom, ask each child to find a stick about the same height as them.
- Find twigs and grasses and tie them securely to the stick. Mount it and fly it through the woods.
- To make a magic potion, have a container such as a large saucepan or 'portable cauldron' (yoghurt pots), or even roll a large leaf into a cone to use.
- Ask the children to find a stirring stick and collect a range of natural things like seeds, grass, leaves and mud, and mix them up in their container.
- Children need to smell their concoction and think of a name for their potion; it could do something exciting like turning you into a fairy or superhero, or making you fly like a bird, but bad potions might change you into a warty toad or smelly socks!
- For special magic, add in some 'magic water'; this could contain some food colouring or even glitter for that extra 'fairy' touch.
- Make some magic spell leaves by drawing patterns and designs on the leaves with metallic-paint pens.
- When the leaves are dry, varnish the leaves with a PVA-glue-and-water mix (three parts glue to one part water).

Teaching tip

Such activities fit in well with stories like Julia Donaldson's *Room on the Broom*, but you can also use different elements like the potion-making as a prelude to the traditional tale 'Stone Soup' before making soup over the fire.

Bonus idea ★

Magic leaves can be used to decorate lots of different items – for example, crowns, an autumn garland, mobiles and display board borders – or you can laminate them or use clear, sticky-backed plastic to make mobiles or bookmarks.

IDEA 38

Conker balance

'The ground at Forest School is covered with conkers. Playing the game "conkers", where you hang them on strings, is not suitable for nursery-aged children.'

Counting, weighing and balancing conkers can make use of abundant free resources to enhance mathematical learning.

There are many things you can do with conkers and acorns, from drawing or sticking googly eyes on them, to making little forest pets or even natural artwork in the style of Andy Goldsworthy.

- Tie some string from the hoop of a coat hanger and hang it from a branch. You can cover the metal end with masking tape or duct tape to make sure it is safe.
- Using two strings of equal length tied on and secured with masking tape, tie identical buckets onto either corner of the hanger. Make sure that it hangs level.
- Collect acorns, conkers, pine cones and pebbles. Use them for weighing and comparing. How many acorns does it take to balance three conkers? How many pine cones do you need to balance a pebble?

There are plenty of other uses for conkers and acorns. These could include:

- Counting them, arranging them, collecting and transporting them, or rolling them down a tube or guttering.
- You could make a slide from a tarpaulin laid on a slope, or bounce them on a tarpaulin in a parachute-type game.
- Use them to make crunchy mud pies or bury them in the soil and they may start to grow into a new tree.
- You could leave a collection of them at the base of a tree, ready for the squirrels to find.

> **Bonus idea** ★
>
> Have an acorn (or conker) and spoon race. Balance one on a spoon and walk with it. Can the children go under something, over something, around a tree and turn in a circle without dropping it? This activity develops good balance and hand-eye coordination.

IDEA 39

Acorn mushrooms

'In the middle of our Forest School area, there is a big oak tree, which produces lots of acorns. The children collect them, sort and count them as well as transporting them to other areas of the woodland.'

Oak trees are a wonderful resource to have at Forest School. Use their fruits to create beautiful mushrooms.

Acorn mushrooms use natural resources to create beautiful objects, which can be used to enhance play or taken home as mini keepsakes.

- Collect the caps from acorns.
- Paint them with poster paints and add on dots and patterns with cotton bud sticks.
- Whittle a twig, about the diameter of a drinking straw, to a point at one end with potato peelers or a whittling knife.
- Fill the acorn cup with air-drying clay and push the twig's blunt end deep into the clay. Push the clay with your fingers to hold the twig firmly.
- Push the acorn cup mushroom into the ground to stand up.
- These make lovely decorations to place around fairy doors and log houses, or you could create a toadstool fairy circle for when the fairies in your wood have a party.

> **Bonus idea** ★
>
> The acorns can be collected and made into squirrel dinners, arranged and displayed on leaf plates. Alternatively, if you draw faces on them with permanent marker pens, they can be acorn babies, to nurture and place in comfy beds. You can also use the caps to make hats for thumb characters. Draw a face on your thumb with a pen (not a permanent one!) and pop on a hat for an instant animated puppet!

IDEA 40

Sycamore seed crafts

'I liked the seed hunt. We got lots in the bucket, then had helicopter races. My favourite bit was when Tracey went up the tree and threw them all in the air and we had to catch them when they fell down.'

Sycamore seeds are always lots of fun when out with children. Hours can be spent watching 'helicopters' whirl down, collecting and arranging the seeds, counting, sharing, ordering and transporting them and using them in natural craft projects.

- Gather lots of sycamore seeds, both singles and doubles.
- Tie a knot at one end of a piece of string and form a small ball of air-drying clay around the knot. Using at least six 'single' sycamore seeds, press them into the clay to make a star shape. Hang it up to dry.
- For a more permanent decoration, use a hot glue gun instead of clay. These make lovely autumnal or even Christmas tree decorations. You could sprinkle on some glitter, or spray silver or gold for a festive feel.
- Use the double seeds to make some sycamore seed dragonflies. Find a twig for your dragonfly's body. You can use the stick as it is or paint it with beautiful colours and leave it to dry. Alternatively, these look lovely when wrapped with coloured wool to make a brightly coloured body for your dragonfly.
- Using air-drying clay or double-sided sticky tape (the sort used to stick carpets and laminates works best), stick on two pairs of double sycamore seeds to make the wings. Paint the seeds for added effect.
- You can hang the dragonflies from some thread to display them or make them into a mobile to take back to the classroom.

Taking it further

Sycamore seeds can also be used to make fairy wings or owl wings and are wonderful for printing with.

IDEA 41

Christmas tree crafts

'I love the magic that begins to creep into the nursery in the run up to Christmas.'

Forest School activities can reflect the seasonal and festival changes throughout the calendar. Here are a few ideas to try out when preparing for Christmas.

Finding new things to make at Christmas outside the classroom can be challenging, especially with the more limited natural resources around.

- Gather the tops of some brackens and ferns (use scissors to do so, as some have very tough stalks and will cut your hands if pulled).
- Using a paint roller, apply green paint to a fern or bracken. Place it paint-side down onto a sheet of paper or card. Place another sheet on top and gently press down and smooth it with a hand or a clean paint roller.
- Remove the top sheet of paper and then carefully peel off the fern. A print of the fern will be left on the paper. Leave it to dry.
- Cut it out and decorate it with sequins and glitter for Christmas cards.
- Create miniature Christmas trees by first gathering a range of small sticks in graduating lengths.
- The longest and straightest stick will be the trunk. Take the second-longest stick and lash it to the first at a right angle on the centre point, about a third of the way up the trunk, to make a cross. Graduate the length of the sticks as you work your way up the 'trunk' stick to form a triangle shape. Decorate with ribbon and beads. If you are taking the tree home, you may want to stick on some sequins and glitter.
- Display by pushing the trunk stick into either the ground or a plant pot.

Teaching tip

Some ferns and bracken can be toxic if eaten. Please ensure that children wash their hands after handling.

Taking it further

You can make an alternative hanging Christmas tree by following the same method but, instead of having a stick branch, use a length of ribbon and just tie each stick centrally with a knot. Leave a small gap between each stick in the graduated triangle to allow for movement.

IDEA 42

Nature plaques

'The children love collecting interesting natural objects to make a museum on a big log at Forest School.'

This is a lovely way to display interesting finds and they also make lovely presents to take home. This is also a great way to demonstrate changing states and chemical reactions to children.

> **Teaching tip**
>
> The adult making the plaster of Paris should wear a dust mask and gloves, as the fine powder has an exothermic reaction when mixed with water and heats up. Keep water nearby to wash off any splashes. Do not pour any leftover plaster away. Leave it to harden, then scrape off and bin. Wipe containers and utensils with a damp cloth.

- Cover the bottom of a shallow container (takeaway containers are great) with sand a few centimetres deep.
- Collect a range of natural objects from your area; acorns, seeds, pine cones, twigs and pine needles work well.
- Arrange your natural treasures in your container, pressing them into the sand.
- An adult needs to make up some plaster of Paris. Do not let the children do this.
- Measure out the water into a mixing container and then sprinkle in the plaster of Paris powder. One cup of water equals two cups of plaster of Paris. Tap the sides of the container to release any air bubbles and then keep adding the powder. Stop adding it when the water does not absorb any more powder and the powder covers the surface of the water. Carefully and gently stir the mixture until it is a smooth consistency. Allow it to stand for a few minutes before pouring it into your sand mould.
- Tap the sides to remove any air bubbles, bend a paperclip outwards and put it into the plaster to make a hanging hook, pressing it in so that just part of the paperclip remains visible.
- Wait until the plaster is fully set and then very carefully turn out the plaque. Use a paintbrush to brush away loose sand. Hang up your plaque by the paperclip hook on the back to display.

IDEA 43

Elder beads

'There is an elder tree in our Forest School area. It's a bit tatty and we are not sure what to do about it.' Head Teacher, Dorset

Make beads from the elder to use in a range of activities, both at Forest School and in the classroom.

Elder trees are a fantastic resource to have in your Forest School area. They benefit from being pruned and tidied up and will send out new shoots when you have done so.

- Using loppers (see Idea 13), cut some elder sticks about the diameter of a 10p piece. Lop them into 'beads' about 3–4 cm long. Do not use pieces that fork or have big knots in.
- The centre of the elder stick is pithy and can easily be pushed out with a tent peg. Do not push the pith out into the palm of your hand.
- The elder bark is easily removed by peeling it off. Leave the bead to dry off for a few minutes and then you can decorate the beads with felt-tip pens or permanent markers. Thread them onto cotton string to make bracelets or necklaces.
- These make lovely natural presents for Mother's Day or the beads can be used to make marionette puppets (see Idea 57). Alternatively, with the addition of some shoelaces, the children can practise threading skills.
- If you make the sticks longer, you have peashooters, whistles or handles for bubble wands (see Idea 53).
- The flowers available in early summer can be used to make elderflower fritters (dip in batter mix and fry) or elderflower cordial (there are lots of recipes in good cookbooks and online). Later, in the autumn, the berries can be used to make jam and syrup.

Taking it further

Elder trees are thought to be magical, so make sure you thank the tree for giving you its branches. Also, if you have a spare phoenix feather, you can try making a wand!

IDEA 44

Leaf ID bunting

'Children ask the names of trees and plants in our area. The adults are not very good at this skill and we spend ages looking up the answers in an ID book.' Nursery Manager, Kent

Knowing what flora and fauna are in your area is important, not only for answering children's questions but also to help with planning what resources you have to hand and those you will need to search further afield for.

Teaching tip

Identify any poisonous plants in the area by mounting these on red card to highlight the fact that children should not touch these.

Taking it further

You can extend this activity by identifying the other plants and flowers in your area and building up a really useful means of identification specific to your area for both staff and children to use.

Bonus idea ★

For flora and fauna that are not possible to laminate, such as minibeasts and fungi, photograph them and laminate the photos instead.

Identification and putting names to things is something that small children will ask for. It is better to prepare in advance and find out what is in your area so that you can answer these questions confidently. Even better, show children how to find out for themselves by having tailored resources for them.

- Visit your Forest School area with a tree identification book, card, paperclips and a pen.
- Using the identification book, choose a tree and find out what it is. Select a leaf from that tree and attach it to some card with a paperclip. Write the name of the tree on the card.
- Continue until you have identified all the different types of trees in your area.
- Return to the classroom and, making sure you have removed any thick stalks, laminate each of the leaves in an individual laminating sheet. Do not forget to include a label with the name of the tree written on both sides.
- Trim them to make triangle-shaped bunting or leave them as rectangles if you prefer. Hole-punch the top of the bunting with a couple of holes and thread through some string or ribbon.
- Display it by stringing the bunting between trees or along a fence. When in your outdoor area, encourage children to try to match leaves that they find with the laminated key.

IDEA 45

Tree cookie blackboards

'The children enjoy mark-making and drawing in the nursery. We would like to extend our provision in the outdoor area to promote writing.' Nursery Manager, Yorkshire

Whiteboards and blackboards are often seen in classrooms and settings as learning tools, but what about outside? Try making this natural alternative. Children will be engaged in creating their own resources to use at Forest School. They also make lovely presents to take home.

- Secure a medium log (at least the width of your forearm) in a saw horse.
- Using a bow saw, make a notch to embed the blade of the saw to stop it bouncing, and then assist the children in cutting slices of wood to make large tree cookies (see Idea 49).
- Using a drill, make a couple of holes at the top of the slice.
- Paint one side of the slice with specialised blackboard paint (available in most DIY shops) and leave it to dry.
- Thread a string through the holes at the top of the slice to hang the blackboard for display.
- Take a packet of chalk with you and let the children start using their handmade resources.

Here are two ways I like to use tree cookies blackboards:

- Why not make a tree cookie blackboard using a log with a larger diameter to make a sign for your Forest School area? The children could decorate it at the beginning of each session to show what their aims are for the session and what they would like to achieve.
- Have a sign-in sheet for each activity where each child could place a tree cookie with their name on to show which activity they are doing.

> **Bonus idea** ★
>
> Use the blackboards to write a menu of what will be served at snack time or cooked on the fire. You can label different areas at Forest School or use it as a learning resource for class answers, mark-making, writing notes to the wildlife, drawing pictures, mud kitchen recipes, forest shop signs, reminders and treasure hunt clues.

IDEA 46

Willow domes

'I visited a school recently and they had a willow dome. When I investigated, they are very much out of our budget.'

Willow structures can enhance any sparse Forest School area or garden by adding fast-growing greenery and form.

If you have access to an established living willow structure, you can build your own willow dome. Willow also grows near rivers and marshes; cutting does not harm it but invigorates growth.

Teaching tip

Always ask permission before helping yourself to cuttings on other people's land.

- Mark out a circle on the ground 2–3 m in diameter. Remove the turf and loosen the soil. Mix in some compost with the loose soil.
- Cut long, straight poles of willow, the thicker the better. Place them into buckets of water to keep fresh until planting.
- Lay out the poles around your prepared circle and push each pole about 30 cm into the ground. Make sure you leave a gap in the circle for a doorway.
- Leave for a month, watering whenever possible. It should take about a month for the poles to start to grow.
- If there are several sprouts from the top of the pole, remove all but the main shoot. Push the cuttings into the ground between each pole. If you plant them at a 45-degree angle, you will eventually be able to weave them into the wall. If any poles do not shoot, pull them up and replace them with new ones.
- When the branches are tall enough, bend them over and tie them to the pole opposite with garden twine. Twist the ends around each other. At the doorway, bend the poles to make an arch and secure with twine.
- Continue to water well (you cannot overwater willow) and encourage any shoots to weave in and out of the other branches.

Taking it further

When your willow dome is well established (after a few years), you will have a ready supply of willow to build other structures, like tunnels and arches, or you could donate the excess willow to other settings to build their own domes.

IDEA 47

Sunflower dens

'We have been looking at willow dens but don't want to build a permanent structure as we are moving to a new building next year.'

This is a spring activity that will grow into a beautiful seasonal den, which will last for a summer at minimal cost. The children will be fascinated at how fast the sunflowers grow.

A sunflower house is a great addition to any setting. The children can watch it grow over a short period of time from a tiny seed to as tall as an adult, and it makes cosy hiding place for imaginative play.

- You will need a packet of sunflower seeds (available from garden centres), an old pencil or dibber, and a ruler.
- If you are planting into grass, you may want to remove a ring of turf to make sure that the children plant the seeds in the right place, or mark it out with string.
- Mark out an area you would like to make into a sunflower den (a circle about 1.5–2 m in diameter is good), making sure you leave space for a doorway.
- Plant sunflower seeds in the ground by making a small hole with a pencil or dibber and putting a seed in and covering it. Plant the seeds around the circle about 30 cm apart (for a circle with a 2 m diameter, you will need approximately 20 seeds).
- Water and, within a couple of weeks, the seeds will have germinated. They will take two to three months to reach full height. They make great hiding places.
- At the end of the season, the sunflower seeds can be harvested and stored to repeat the activity the following spring, to eat (check for food allergies), to feed to pets such as rabbits or hamsters, or to feed to birds in the winter.

Teaching tip

Make sure to check for allergies prior to doing this activity.

Taking it further

You could plant several sunflower circles and make a village, a winding path or a maze for the children to play in.

Bonus idea ★

Seeds can be planted in small pots or egg trays and observed in the classroom until germinated, before transferring outside when established.

IDEA 48

Growing trees

'A society grows great when old men plant trees whose shade they know they shall never sit in.' Anonymous Greek proverb

Connecting children with nature can start from very early childhood; children can help grow and nurture your Forest School space as well as exploring how living things grow.

Teaching children about environmental stewardship and looking after their world can have long-term benefits for society. Although your current children may not see an immediate benefit from planting seeds, they will remember they are there and maybe even visit them when they are adults with their own children, many years later.

- Collect nuts from woodland visits.
- Look for alder cones, pine cones, acorns, beech nuts, sweet chestnuts and hazelnuts. You can also plant apple seeds, pear seeds, plum stones and cherry stones.
- Check that acorns, hazelnuts and beech nuts are good by popping them into a bowl of water. Any that float will not germinate, so you can discard them.
- Fruit seeds and stones are best put in cold conditions, like a fridge, in a zip top bag with slightly damp compost for a couple of weeks before planting. This also works well for hazelnuts.
- Fill yoghurt pots or plant pots with compost.
- Plant the seeds and stones a few centimetres below the surface (seeds from cones can just be placed on the surface) and label the pots. Store them in a shady spot until springtime.
- When they start to germinate, water them to make sure they do not dry out.
- Transplant them to the soil when they are about 25 cm tall, and put compost around the base to encourage growth.

> **Teaching tip**
>
> If other settings near you have different trees, why not do a nut swap?

> **Involving parents**
>
> Grow a sapling for each child and let them take it home with them to plant in either their garden or another outdoor space, so they can visit it and watch the growth throughout their lives.

> **Taking it further**
>
> If you do this every year, you should have trees at different stages of growth in your Forest School area for children to compare their age and height. The Woodland Trust give out tree packs of hedgerow trees most years, which are available free to schools and settings.

ized=# Part 5

Sticks and plants

IDEA 49

Tree cookies

'I made a medal for my mummy because she is my hero and I love her.'

Making tree cookies – or medals – is a multisensory activity that gives even the smallest children a great sense of accomplishment. It is physical, noisy and vibrates their hands, and freshly cut wood gives off a lovely aroma.

Teaching tip

Use tree cookies for counting, letter recognition, matching games and pairs. Leaves or pictures stuck and sealed with some varnish can be used for identification games or storytelling starters. You can stick on pictures from a story and use them for sequencing events or as prompts for acting out a story.

Bonus idea ★

Drill a hole in the centre of one tree cookie and poke a fir twig into it to make a mini Christmas tree. Or, by drilling lots of them, you can make an articulated caterpillar!

This activity is great for learning to use tools but also for creating resources to use at Forest School.

- Place a long length of wood at least 6 cm in diameter into the saw horse or secure it in a low fork of a tree. Use clamps if necessary.
- Pre-cut a groove into the wood 0.5–1 cm in from the end, and embed the bow saw blade so that it doesn't bounce or slip.
- Position the child so that both of their hands are on the handle of the saw and help them to practise the pushing and pulling motion with their arms to saw through the wood to make a tree cookie.
- Placing the cookie onto a flat surface, drill a hole near the top to hang a string from.
- Decorate it with felt-tip pens, paints, charcoal or by sticking sequins on. Make medals for prizes or as name tags.
- Tree cookies can be used as a basis for many Forest School activities. Why not have a collection, along with some hazel stick cylinders about 5 cm long, for the children to use as building blocks for construction?

IDEA 50

Bell shaker

'I like making music in the forest. The squirrels liked it too.' Three-year-old girl, Cornwall

Children, music and dancing go hand in hand. Exploring rhythms and movement, along with working with others, becomes a whole-body memory, and children will often recall the joyous experience. This activity can become part of a festive celebration.

These simple shakers are colourful, noisy and easy to make and will encourage dancing and movement to complement any song you love singing together.

- Help the children to find a forked stick each, no thinner than a pencil. You may need to use loppers (see Idea 13) to make the ends of the stick safe.
- Have pre-cut lengths of colourful ribbon and wool available and show the children how to tie them onto their sticks.
- Wind the wool and ribbons around the sticks to make them colourful, beautiful and soft to hold.
- Tie a piece of string to one of the forks of the stick and thread on some bells. You can easily buy them online or in pound shops, especially in the run up to Christmas.
- Tie the other end of the string to the other prong of the forked stick.
- Shake the stick to make a jingling sound
- These can be used at any time of the year to make music outside, but they make especially lovely Christmas accessories for festive music-making and for accompanying singing.

> **Involving parents**
>
> Make these bell shakers with the children and have a festive Forest School day in the woods with parents and families. Hot chocolate with marshmallows around a campfire, while the children sing Christmas songs accompanied by their instruments, will make a very special end-of-term celebration for families.

> **Bonus idea** ★
>
> Make crowns with card and double-sided sticky tape (the type available from carpet shops is ideal as it is stronger). Decorate with leaves, grasses and natural resources found at Forest School, for a natural costume to complement the musical activities and make the children feel very special for the occasion.

IDEA 51

Simple dreamcatchers

'I think it had a bad dream, flew out of its nest, hit its head on a tree and died.' Small child when we found a dead bird in the woods

After this sad event, we made some dreamcatchers to hang in our Forest School area to protect the birds and animals from bad dreams.

Native American dreamcatchers originate from the Ojibwa (Chippewa) tribe, who believed that the dreamcatchers were the webs of a good spider, who let good dreams pass through the holes and caught bad dreams in its threads. These bad dreams would disappear as soon as the sun rose.

- Cut a long stick of willow (known as a whip). If willow is not available, you can use thin, bendy twigs or gardening wire.
- Make a loop with a willow whip and tie it with string. To add colour and decoration, wrap wool around the diameter of the hoop. This also helps to hold it securely.
- Using a contrasting string or wool, create a spider's web by crisscrossing the hoop with thread. Before you finish, thread on a bead to represent the spider, then secure to finish.
- Tie a loop of thread to the top to hang it up and add some more threads to the bottom. Thread some beads and feathers and any other small natural objects you can find on to these strings.
- Hang your dreamcatchers from tree branches to protect the woodland creatures from bad dreams, or let the children take them home to hang by their beds to keep their dreams sweet.

Bonus idea ★

Combine this activity with storytelling to explore other cultures and traditional stories. Talk about dreams that the children may have had and how the dreamcatchers will keep the bad dreams away.

IDEA 52

Log houses

'My house is where the fairies live. I put it in the woods with the other houses and it looks like a little town. The fairies will be happy there.'

Exploring the range of homes and houses is a common topic in the Early Years. Make your Forest School area into your local village, town or city to reflect the homes of the children.

Introduce this activity by talking about the different types of homes that people can live in. Find out what sort of houses the children live in. Do they live in a house, a flat, a cottage, a caravan? Think about the common features of homes – for example, windows and doors – as well as features that make our homes individual.

- Collect some suitable logs. You may want to split them in advance so that they have flat faces.
- Scatter them around your area for the children to find and choose which one they would like to use. Make sure that you have at least one split log per child. Any leftovers can be used at another time or as fuel for the fire.
- Provide a range of art and craft materials, such as felt, craft matchsticks, sequins, buttons, cotton wool, paint and fabric.
- Give the children the opportunity to design and decorate their log to make a house. You may want to use longer logs to make tower blocks or larger buildings to reflect the type of housing that the children live in.
- This activity works well with projects about homes and buildings. You can make a village, town or city of houses, or use them as fairy homes.

Teaching tip

Some children live in non-conventional homes. If you have caravan dwellers, for example, you may want to offer tree cookies (Idea 49) for wheels in the resources you provide, so that these children have the opportunity to make their home if they would like.

IDEA 53

Elder bubble wands

'Making their own bubble wands and producing their own bubble mixture involved lots of maths, measuring, design technology and chemistry and was so much fun that the children didn't even realise they were learning! We will definitely revisit this activity again.'

Activities that incorporate lots of skills and curriculum areas hit many targets, and this one is lovely to do as a group activity. Children enjoy making and using their own resources.

Teaching tip

To make a simple bubble mixture, gently mix 1 l of hot water with 250 ml of quality washing-up liquid (cheap, runny washing-up liquid doesn't work very well). Stir in four tablespoons of glycerine, available in supermarket cake-making aisles, chemists or online, and leave to cool. Decant into pots and use to blow bubbles with your elder bubble wands. Beware of bubble mixture getting near eyes and have a bucket of water available to wash soapy hands.

Many children are bubble fanatics, and this activity was developed to take their enjoyment a little bit further and extend their learning by drawing on their natural love of bubble-making.

- Using loppers (see Idea 13), cut some elder sticks 10–20 cm long. With a metal tent peg, push out the pith in the centre of the stick. This will form the bubble wand handle.
- Cut a piece of wire three times the length of the handle (caution is needed when using wire cutters), fashion a loop in the centre of the wire and twist the wire to secure.
- Thread on some beads (wooden ones look particularly nice but any chunky beads that are bigger than the elder pith hole will do).
- Thread the wires through the elder handle and add another bead at the base of the wand. Wrap the wire around the bead and push it back through so that the ends of the wire are secured within the elder handle. Make sure all wire ends are tucked inside the handle to prevent scratches.
- You can bind the handle with coloured thread for added decoration.

IDEA 54

Fairy doors

'The girls in our setting are very interested in fairies and spend a lot of time at Forest School searching for evidence of them.'

There is nothing quite as magical as letting your imagination roam in the world of fairies. A great starting point is making the Forest School area fairy-friendly by making fairy doors so they can live in the grounds.

Children are often fascinated by the world of fairies and pixies, and it can be linked to many traditional tales to promote literacy. Extend children's interests by making Forest School a welcoming place for magical folk.

- To make fairy doors, collect together a range of small, straight sticks of similar length. You can trim them with secateurs (alternatively, use craft lollipop sticks).
- Fashion a small door by placing the sticks side by side, using a cross bar to hold them all in place. Use string or glue to fix them together.
- Alternatively, you can make tree cookies (see Idea 49) from an oval-shaped log and cut off one end to give it a flat base.
- Find natural materials to decorate your door and find a suitable hollow in the base of a tree to rest your door against.
- You may want to decorate the area by making a small garden path and garden. Try making a small window to complement your door and add more doors to other trees to make your outdoor area into fairyland.
- Small ladders made with string and twigs and hung in trees also encourage children's imaginative play. Use them along with stick fairies to encourage children in their small-person, imaginative and animistic play.

> **Bonus idea** ★
>
> Colouring sugar to make fairy trails can add to the magic and is not harmful to the environment. Add liquid food colouring to some granulated sugar in a bowl, mix well and then spread out on a tray and leave to dry for a couple of hours. When dry, break up any lumps and pop into a bag, ready to sprinkle around the fairy doors (on a dry day) for evidence that the fairies have been visiting.

IDEA 55

Willow lanterns

'We have been exploring light with our preschoolers at nursery and would like to extend this to Forest School.'

Light is a great choice of topic, with lots of possibilities when outside. Lanterns are easy to make and very effective, especially for parades and celebration sessions in the winter months when it gets dark early.

Making lanterns can complement many different occasions, from carol singing to the Chinese New Year. They are easy to make, using both natural and classroom resources and a little bit of adult assistance.

- Cut some willow sticks. If using dried willow, soak it first.
- To make a cube lantern, cut 24 willow sticks at 30 cm long and ten at 43 cm long.
- Make six squares from the shorter sticks. Join the corners together using masking tape.
- Make a cross from the longer willow sticks and join them to five of the squares, from corner to corner, to make the squares more rigid.
- On one of the squares, attach a metal jar lid to the cross, using strong double-sided tape or wire. This will hold the light and will be the base of your lantern.
- Put the squares together to form a cube. If the square with the lid forms the base, then the square without a cross should be one of the sides.
- Add a long string loop to the top of the cube.
- Using PVA glue, paint the willow sticks on the outside surface and gently press craft tissue paper squares (or tracing paper cut to size) to the sticks to make the sides. Do not do this on the side without the cross.

Taking it further

Experiment with making different-shaped lanterns, like square-based pyramids, cuboids, spheres and stars. This also works effectively with glow sticks.

- Leave it to dry and then decorate the lanterns by gluing dry autumn leaves to the tracing or tissue paper.
- Make an extra tissue square and attach it only to the top stick of the square side that does not contain a cross.
- Hang the lantern from the end of a stick. Secure it with masking tape.
- Using the side panel for access, put a tealight candle or a battery-operated one into the metal dish and secure it with some double-sided tape. Light it (or switch it on).
- Secure the tissue paper 'wall' to the bottom of the square with some masking tape.
- Hold the end of the stick to carry the lantern.

> **Bonus idea** ★
>
> Invite the children to stick cardboard shapes to the tissue paper and explore the shadows created.

IDEA 56

Forest friends and mini dens

'Small-people play in our nursery is very popular. Children use their imagination and work cooperatively to build imaginary play worlds for the pieces.'

Activities such as small-world play promote cooperation and problem solving, as well as giving children the opportunity to try out ideas in the safe environment of it being 'another person' rather than themselves. Making their own figures can help children to create their own ideas of persona and ideal self.

In the context of small-world play, children build on their own experiences, act out past events and build on their imaginative skills, as well as developing vocabulary and using it in context. They play alongside each other as well as developing the ability to work cooperatively with others.

- Using loppers, help the children to cut a stick about 15 cm long.
- Holding one end of the stick, use a knife or potato peeler to remove the bark from the top 3 cm of the other end.
- Draw on a face with felt-tip pens and, using either natural materials or some scraps of fabric, tie on some clothes. To extend the children's learning, you may want to show them how to lash on some arms.
- A couple of leaves can transform the figure into a fairy, or a fabric cloak can make a superhero. If the end of the stick is whittled into a point and coloured in, you have a gnome or even a Santa. Silky light blue fabric can be used to make a princess or camouflage fabric can make soldiers.
- Design and build a home for fairies, superheroes or woodland characters, using only natural materials to make sure that they will be cosy and comfortable in their home. Think about keeping them dry and warm.

Taking it further

This activity works with children of all ages and can fit in with class themes. We have made fairy homes, wattle and daub mini houses, luxury penthouse apartments, a Viking longhouse, tepees, an elf hospital (National Elf Service), a Norman castle, Hampton Court Palace and a survivor camp. We have made a woodland nativity scene and re-enacted the stories of the Three Little Pigs and Rama and Sita.

- Once their basic needs are met, what else could you add to make life in their home more comfortable or fun?
- Encourage the children to work with others and talk about the story behind this home. Who lives there? Who do they live with?
- This activity promotes lots of imaginative play amongst children, and these simple resources can be used for hours of play and explorations.

> **Bonus idea** ★
>
> Use acorn cups and air-drying clay to make fairy cups and saucers when children are having tea parties in the woods with their forest friend fairies. What other accessories could you make using natural resources? Perhaps a tree cookie table, acorn cup stools or twig chairs.

IDEA 57

Marionette puppets

'We would like to develop puppet play as our children, especially the reluctant talkers, respond well when using them.'

This activity can be done over the course of a few sessions, or all in one go if you prepare some of the resources before the session.

Using puppets helps to promote social and emotional development, teaches conversation skills and social behaviours, and develops children's empathy with others.

- Cut two tree cookies (see Idea 49) for each child, ideally one with a smaller diameter for a head and one with a larger diameter for the body.
- Drill two holes in the head cookie, one at the top and one at the bottom. Drill five holes in the body cookie, one for the neck and one for each of the limbs.
- Cut some elder sticks about the diameter of a ten-pence piece. Lop them into pieces about 3–4 cm long. The centre of the elder stick is pithy and can easily be pushed out with a tent peg.
- Tie a bead onto the end of a string for a shoe. Thread on a long elder stick and attach it to the body. Repeat with the other limbs.
- Attach the body to the head with a piece of string.
- Make a cross from a couple of sticks. Run a string from the top of the head to the centre of the stick. Tie a string from the hands to opposite sides of the cross. Waggle the cross from side to side to wave the arms.
- Why not make up a play together or take your puppets for a walk around your outdoor site?

Taking it further

Extend activity by making articulated limbs. Make lower and upper legs with separate elder beads and then tie strings from the centre of each leg (the 'knees') to each end of another stick. Work the legs by tilting the stick to lift the knees and make a stepping motion. You can do the same with the arms. With a bit of practice, you can make your puppets move and interact with each other.

Bugs and minibeasts

Part 6

IDEA 58

Umbrella bug-catching

'Our children are fascinated with minibeasts and bug-hunting. Sometimes we find loads but other times it can be difficult to find any at all, which is quite frustrating.' Preschool Practitioner, Devon

Searching for and observing minibeasts is something that fascinates both children and adults alike and builds a respect for other living creatures.

Small children love hunting for bugs. They are a great learning resource for matching, comparing, counting and looking at different features of living creatures up close.

- Provide the children with bug-collecting apparatus, such as collecting pots and a magnifying glass, and allow them access to an identification aid, such as ID charts and books, to identify what you have found. It is also a good idea to have a camera to record findings.
- Look in cool, dark places such as under logs and stones, in the crevices of trees and under leaves on bushes.
- An easy method of bug-collecting that works well is to hold an open umbrella upside down under a bush, tree or hedge and shake the branches vigorously for about 30 seconds. An array of minibeasts will drop into the inverted umbrella, and they can then be tipped into the collecting pots for closer scrutiny.
- Be careful about touching insects and bugs, as some (especially the hairy ones) may cause skin irritation.
- When you have finished looking at the bugs you have collected, return them to the locations where you found them.

Teaching tip

There is a vast range of bug-hunting identification resources available to use. Check out www.naturedetectives.org.uk for simple ID sheets, or look at ID charts from the Field Studies Council (www.field-studies-council.org/publications).

Bonus idea ★

Using air-drying clay and natural resources, create your own minibeasts. Twigs can be bodies and legs, leaves and sycamore seeds can be wings and pine needles or grass heads can represent antennae. Use seed heads or small stones for eyes. Talk to the children about the habitats that the bugs might like to live in and what they might like to eat.

IDEA 59

Peg caterpillars

'He ate through some nice green leaves and then he felt much better.' – Eric Carle, *The Very Hungry Caterpillar*

Many Early Years settings have a range of books and resources to explore animal life cycles, and this topic is a great introduction to scientific investigation for young children.

Life cycles of different creatures are fascinating for children. These next few activities are designed for when you are exploring butterflies.

- Talk to the children and find out what they already know about caterpillars. Has anyone seen one? What did it look like? What colour was it? Did it have patterns?
- Collect some wooden spring pegs and paint them green, brown or patterned, with paints, felt-tips or crayons. Draw on some eyes.
- Take the children for a walk to look for some tasty leaves for the caterpillars to eat. Demonstrate to the children how the caterpillars can wriggle along a branch or twig to find the juiciest leaves.
- Show the children how to squeeze the two ends of the peg together using their forefinger and thumb to open and close the mouth, and how to 'munch' the leaves. Ask the children what they think the caterpillar's favourite food is. Does it prefer green leaves or brown leaves? Does it like daisy petals or buttercups? Why do they think the caterpillars need to eat so much food? Is the reason they eat lots of food to grow, give them energy and keep them healthy?
- You can talk about the life cycle of the caterpillar, starting from a small egg, hatching into a caterpillar, pupating and then emerging into a butterfly.

Teaching tip

This is also a really good exercise for young children to develop finger muscles for pre-writing skills. For children who are not yet showing a dominant writing hand, you may want to encourage them to alternate hands or have a 'caterpillar' in each hand to work.

Taking it further

Write numbers on the caterpillars and ask the children to give the caterpillars the right number of leaves, or decorate them with different colours and patterns and ask the children to find leaves that match (light green, dark green, yellow, brown, orange, stripy, specked, etc.).

IDEA 60

Butterfly petal-bashing

'Wow, just wow!' Early Years pupil

This is a great activity to show how colours from plants can be transferred onto watercolour paper with the Japanese art technique of *Hapa Zome*.

Explore the symmetry of butterfly wings by using plants and flowers to create beautiful patterns and colours.

- Use a sheet of watercolour paper and fold it in half. Open out the paper and, on one half, lay out a range of small leaves and flower petals.
- Refold the paper and lay it on a firm, flat surface. Tap the paper all over with a hammer or mallet. The more tapping, the better the results.
- Open the paper and remove any leftover bits of petals and leaves. The colours from the plant material should transfer to the paper.
- Fold the paper over again and cut out butterfly-shaped wings. Find a long, straight stick and use it as the butterfly's body; attach it with glue or double-sided sticky tape (double-sided carpet tape available from DIY stores works very well for outdoor activities, as it is strong enough to hold most natural materials).
- Make sure the stick is long enough to extend below the wings, so that the children can hold the end of the stick as a handle and take the butterflies for a flutter around your Forest School area.
- This activity also works really well with cotton-based material (a great use for old sheets).

Taking it further

If you have made the peg caterpillars (Idea 59), you could use the pegs as the butterfly's body for continuity to demonstrate the life cycle of a butterfly. A small child's sock works as a cocoon; fill the other sock with a pre-prepared butterfly. This works best with butterflies made from material rather than paper, as you can roll them up and pop them in the sock. Use these visual resources to explore the whole process of the life cycle of a butterfly with your class.

Bonus idea ★

Have a go at cutting out cotton material into triangles and make some Forest School bunting using the same method.

IDEA 61

Threading caterpillars

'Look at how many leaves this greedy caterpillar has eaten.'
– Eric Carle, *The Very Hungry Caterpillar*

Investigating the types of food eaten by minibeasts can help children understand the importance of looking after the natural environment, to provide habitats and food sources for other living creatures.

Continue exploring the caterpillar theme by making some pipe cleaner caterpillars. Threading is an important skill for hand–eye coordination and for developing finger muscles for writing.

- Each child needs a pipe cleaner. Tie one end of a length of wool to the middle of the pipe cleaner. Fold the pipe cleaner in half and twist it to make a stiff caterpillar.
- Tie a small stick to the end of the wool to stop the leaves falling off the end.
- Collect a range of leaves of different colours and shapes. Try to ensure that they are reasonably fresh, as this activity will not work very well with dry, crumbly leaves.
- Using a hole punch or a pointed stick, make two holes in each leaf. Ask the children to select some of the leaves with holes in.
- Carefully poke the end of the pipe cleaner caterpillar through each hole; gently push the leaf down the wool so that it lays flat.

Involving parents

This is a great activity to include in story sacks with *The Hungry Caterpillar* book by Eric Carle. The children can then demonstrate to their parents how caterpillars eat. You may want to make some felt leaves if the story sacks go home for extended periods, or ask the families to collect leaves from their gardens or local park.

Taking it further

These caterpillars and leaves make lovely classroom displays. Add some thread to make caterpillar mobiles. You can glue on some googly eyes or eye stickers to complete it. How about writing the letters of the child's name on the leaves with marker pens?

IDEA 62

Snail racing

'The children were really engaged with collecting the snails from our vegetable garden and later racing them in the Forest School area, which then became the new home for all the snail racers.' Teacher

Snail racing is an exciting activity despite its slow pace, and children become very proud of their snails as well as offering encouragement to other snails in the race.

As well as being an activity I am sure the children will want to revisit again and again, snail racing also helps the children learn to offer encouragement to others.

- Collect snails from your outdoor area. Damp places are best for snail hunting. Give the children a bug-collecting container or buckets. Put some damp leaves in the container to ensure that the snails do not dry out.
- Give each child – or 'snail team' if you can't find enough for one snail each – a small sticker and pens, and let them decide on their snail's name and racing colours and decorate the sticker accordingly.
- Pop the sticker onto the top of the snail shell for ease of identification when the race starts.
- Dip a small sheet or tablecloth into a bucket of water and spread it out on the ground.
- Place the snails on the sheet and add some lovely green leaves or other tasty delights at the end and start the race. Snails particularly like cucumber, tomatoes, lettuce, carrot peelings and cabbage leaves.
- Lots of verbal encouragement and cheering for the snails is recommended.
- If the sheet is drying out, you can spray or lightly water it with a watering can to keep it moist. Snails prefer it damp and will tend to retreat into their shells if the surface becomes too dry for them.
- The first snail to reach the food is the winner.

Teaching tip

Return the snails to the wild after the race but please ensure that you remove the stickers first, as the stickers make them more easily spotted by birds.

Bonus idea ★

We made some little trophies for our snails out of acorn cups filled with mango bits (from our snack box), but the prizes are up to you. Snails like eating most fruit and salad vegetables.

IDEA 63

Bug stones

'The children love minibeast hunting and we are looking for a simple activity to complement this.' Early Years Practitioner, Swindon

Recreate the colours, patterns and features you have observed on minibeasts found in your outdoor area to make your own bug gang.

Using just the resources found in your Forest School area, with a few items from the classroom, this is a great craft activity which can be repeated throughout the year.

- Collect a range of smooth stones or pebbles. If your area does not have any suitable stones, it is possible to buy a sack of pebbles in garden centres and DIY stores.
- Decorate the stones with drawings of bugs and minibeasts. Using chalks and charcoal means that the colours will wash off if left outside in the rain (pastels will last longer than chalks and provide more vivid colours but are less environmentally friendly). Alternatively, you can wash the stones to make them reusable for other groups and occasions.
- Oval pebbles with red chalk and black charcoal can easily be transformed into ladybirds. Using yellow chalk and black charcoal, the same stone could be a bee.
- Make a bug parade by arranging the bug stones in a line. Use them for counting, sorting, building mini den homes, exploring habitats, etc.
- You can try using several stones to make a minibeast; how about using small pebbles in a row to make a caterpillar or a round pebble balanced on top of a long stone to make a snail with its shell?
- Take water to wash hands after this activity as it can be quite messy.

> **Bonus idea** ★
>
> Make five ladybirds and five bees, then draw a grid with nine squares using sticks – now you can play minibeast noughts and crosses!

IDEA 64

Sticky spider's web

'Today we played Incy Wincy Spider and helped the spider to catch bugs in his web. He thought they were delicious!'

This activity not only deepens children's knowledge and understanding about spiders but also helps to develop their throwing skills.

Most spiders are carnivorous and eat other insects and animals. They make webs and egg sacs from spider silk, which they make in their spinneret glands in their abdomens. Spider's silk is very strong and the spider can detect when something is caught in its web by vibrations.

- Using masking tape (sticky paper tape), construct a spider's web between two trees. Make sure that the sticky side of the tape is all facing in the same direction.
- Each player needs to select some alder cones and decorate them with coloured wool to represent bugs. If you do not have access to alder cones, small scrunched up newspaper balls also work well.
- Decide on a standing point approximately half a metre away from the web (sticky side facing you) and take it in turns to throw the 'bugs' at the web. The winner is the person who manages to stick the most bugs to the web.
- When you have finished the activity, remove all the tape from the trees and dispose of it responsibly.

Teaching tip

Search for webs on hedgerows; they can be made more visible by spraying them with a fine mist from a water bottle. To 'catch' a spider web for closer observation, carefully bend a willow rod into a grapefruit-sized loop and tie with string. Gently try to scoop the web onto your hoop – it should stick to the willow. If it's sunny, hold it above a sheet of card and look at the delicate shadow it casts.

Bonus idea ★

Make a willow wand for each child and use string or wool to create a web. Let them decorate the web with grass and leaves.

Mud and weather

Part 7

IDEA 65

Making mud paint

'I like this sort of paint best. Can we use it in nursery?' Four-year-old child

There is nothing quite like playing with mud and using it for mark-making. Mixing mud with different amounts of water to change the consistency will also show the children how to experiment through trial and error to reach a workable product.

Experimenting as scientists to make their own resources to complete a task always fascinates children.

Teaching tip

Talk to the children about their ideas and ask them to form their own hypotheses about how to make resources from the Forest School. Then let them experiment using trial and error to perfect their paint and brushes.

- The resources you will need for this idea are mixing pots, pestles and mortars (try charity shops), PVA glue, water, paintbrushes, card and mud.
- Collect some mud from your outdoor area. Mix it with some water and a drop of PVA glue and paint it onto a piece of card. Does it go on smoothly or is it lumpy?
- Next, put some more mud into a mortar and grind it as finely as you can with a pestle. Alternatively, you can use smooth pebbles as grinders. Again, mix it with some water and PVA to make a paint-like consistency and try painting again. Compare and contrast the two paints: why do the children think that there is a difference in the quality of the paints?
- Try with different colour soils (collect from different areas) or different colour clays. Classroom clay that has dried out or crumbled is great for this activity. The added PVA helps the mixture to stay on the card and not flake off so easily when dried.
- Once you have made your mud paint, you then need to decide how you want to paint with it. You could try using a classroom paintbrush or perhaps some decorating brushes or even just a stick.

Bonus idea ★

Try making your own brushes to experiment with. Find a twig and, using masking tape or elastic bands, affix some natural brushes to the handle. Try grass, flower heads, tiny twigs, moss or leaves. Pine needles create an interesting, bristly effect and feathers a fine, sweeping effect. Don't forget that fingers are great for painting with too!

IDEA 66

Mud painting

'Nan doesn't like mud in her house but she will love this.'

Mark-making with child-made resources opens up a wide range of activities to try, and may spark off ideas as the children embrace their roles as experimenters and inventors.

Now you have your mud paint (see Idea 65) and tools to paint with, you will need to decide what you are going to paint.

Mud postcards
- Give each child a postcard-sized piece of card and let them paint their favourite activity at Forest School using the resources that they made earlier.

Flag painting
- Give the children some material, ideally cotton-based, and let them use mud to design a flag or some bunting to decorate your Forest School area.

Leaf printing
- Paint leaves with mud paint and press them down onto material or card. This will show up the shape and features of the leaf.
- Make a collage of all the different types of leaves in your outdoor area, perhaps identifying them and learning the names of the trees and plants they came from.

Totem poles
- If you are looking at other cultures or beliefs, how about making a totem pole? Many shops that sell carpets and material are very happy for you to have the leftover cardboard tubes.
- Drive a large pole or stake into the ground and place the carpet tube over it to keep it upright.
- Let the children paint the tube to make a totem pole.
- Add on eyes, ears, noses and beaks to make the totem relevant to your group.

Teaching tip

Give the totem pole a coat of clear varnish, including the top and bottom edges, to semi-waterproof it.

IDEA 67

Mud bricks

'We will be learning about the story of the Three Little Pigs and have built some stick homes and grass houses. Apart from plastic building bricks, we cannot find anything to make brick houses from.'

This activity is useful when looking at building, construction and homes, but also works well as an additional play resource. Make lots of bricks so the children have plenty of resources to enable them to complete their projects.

Teaching tip

If you do not have access to clay, you can try adding in some PVA glue to the mud mixture to strengthen the bricks.

Taking it further

Make a wall from twigs and willow interwoven with each other and cover it in a mud-and-clay mix to make wattle and daub walls.

- Collect some mud from just under the surface and break it up into a fine, crumbly mixture. Remove any lumps, debris and stones. You can use sieves to do this if you have any.
- If you have clay, pop some into a bucket and mix it well with the mud, as this will make the bricks stronger, and then add some water to bind it. If you do not have clay available, just mix the mud you have into a traditional mud-pie mix using water. Do not make the mixture too wet.
- Press the mixture into ice cube trays. Tap the ice cube trays on the ground to remove any air bubbles.
- Stand the trays in the sun for a little while, and then carefully turn out and leave the bricks to dry in the sun. If possible, turn the bricks to dry them on all sides.
- Use the bricks for building houses and walls. You can even mix up 'concrete' with mud and water to stick the bricks together.

IDEA 68

Pitter patter flood!

'Our children like playing group games and are just starting to learn how to follow rules.'

Role-playing different animals can be a good introduction to help children develop their imaginative play and pretend to be something other than themselves.

Simple, repetitive games with easy-to-follow rules are good for Early Years children to develop their listening and cooperation skills.

- Find a spot in your Forest School area with logs and low tree branches, forks in trees and with slightly higher ground, such as slopes or mounds.
- Ask the children to all mime a named animal. First, you might want to ask them to be squirrels scampering; on the next turn, you may want to ask them to be slithery snakes or snuffling hedgehogs.
- Have everyone moving around your area, acting the movements of the named animal. Don't forget to join in yourself!
- Suddenly stop, put your hands to your ears and say, 'Pitter patter, pitter patter, it's raining!'.
- Then say, 'Pitter patter, pitter patter, flood!'. Everyone has to get their feet off the ground. This could be jumping on a log, dangling from a branch or climbing up into the low fork of a tree. They can also go up slopes or stand on a rock or a mound.
- Look at the ground and say, 'Phew, the water has gone,' and ask everyone to come down to ground level again.
- Play again, this time being a different animal. When the children have played a few times, let them take it in turns to choose an animal and be the person who shouts 'Flood!'.

Teaching tip

This is a great way to introduce new animals to children and explore the way they look and move. This extends their knowledge and vocabulary as well as being a good way to get children moving, especially on a cold day to keep them warm.

Bonus idea ★

'Crocodiles' is another good moving game. Find a clear area and lay out rope buses in circles on the ground. Show the children how to pretend to swim and splash in the water. Shout out 'Crocodiles!' and everybody has to jump onto a rope island to keep safe.

IDEA 69

Rain painting

'When it is raining at Forest School, we rarely do any activities except puddle splashing and mud mixing. I always feel it's a wasted opportunity but what can we do in wet weather?'

Being outside in the rain gives us another resource to experiment with . . . if the rain was an artist, what would its pictures look like?

Rainy days are happy, splashy days according to my five-year-old son, who likes nothing better than playing and going for walks in the rain. This is a great time to put up a tarpaulin shelter in your Forest School area. Large tarpaulins are available from DIY shops. Fix a rope between two trees and drape a tarpaulin over it then peg down to make an easy temporary shelter for a refuge from the rain during sessions.

- Lay paper on the ground and use pebbles or stones to weigh the corners of the paper down. If the ground is wet, lay down a small tarpaulin first to work on.
- Splodge some paint or food colouring onto the paper and let the rain do the work. The rain water will spread and mix the colours.
- Try this activity with powder paint by sprinkling dry powder paint onto the paper, and then watch as the paint dissolves in the raindrops.
- When you are happy with the end result, move the finished painting to a covered area and leave to dry. If you hang the paper up vertically, you can get some interesting dribble effects.

Taking it further

If you would like to make a large group painting, try using a roll of wall lining paper and sprinkle powder paint on it – you will get some good effects. If you want to keep the artwork, remove it to a dry area. When it is dry, it makes really lovely wrapping paper or backing paper for nursery displays about the weather or Forest School activities.

IDEA 70

Rainstorm music

'Some of our children get so excited when we are outside if it rains; all they want to do is jump around, while others want to do more focused activities.'

Making our own rainstorm can focus children on the rhythms and sounds that can be heard in nature, as well as making music using different parts of our bodies. It can also be a great introduction to science and the water cycle.

The group stands in a circle or sits around the fire pit. They need to be quiet and focused for this activity to be really effective.

- The leader makes a noise that sounds like light raindrops by tapping a finger on the palm of their hand continually. They 'pass' the sound to the next person in the circle, who continues making this sound.
- The next person in the circle makes the same sound then turns and passes it to the person standing next to them. This continues all the way around the circle, with everybody joining in making the noise so that it gets louder and louder.
- When the last person in the circle has been passed the sound, the leader changes the sound to something louder, such as a hand clap, foot stamp, stomach tap or tongue click.
- Do multiple sounds until it is really noisy, just like a tropical rainstorm. Then reduce the sounds until there is silence.
- After the activity, reflect with the children on how they felt about the rainstorm and the noises they made.

Bonus idea ★

This also works as a worm-charming activity – when doing this outside (especially when it is damp or raining), we have observed lots of earthworms on the ground where we had been gathered, especially if tapping, stamping feet and jumping has been part of the rainstorm music. Collect worms found in the area in a jar to observe more closely, but return them to the soil again after the activity.

IDEA 71

Wind drawing

'We love being outside when the wind is rustling the leaves and we imagine being by the sea with the sound of the waves. We often wonder what the wind is saying.'

What if you could see what the wind looks like? What if the wind could draw? This is a lovely way for Early Years children to compare their drawing style with that of the wind.

Harness the energy of the wind to make some stunning visual displays to remind the children of how it felt being in the wind.

- On a breezy day, when the leaves are rustling, find a tree with some low-hanging branches.
- Tie some string to the end of some of the thinnest twigs at the ends of the branches, and make sure that the string almost reaches the ground.
- Place some thick paper or card on the ground and tape felt-tip pens to the end of the string so that the nibs are just touching the paper. If it is quite breezy, you will need to put some stones on the corner of the paper to stop it from blowing away.
- Let the wind blow and it will move the pen to make marks on the paper.
- This works particularly well if you have a weeping willow tree.
- Can the children draw like a tree? Try dangling pens from string onto paper.
- Try it with paintbrushes and paint too for some artwork with a difference.
- Try making brushes out of twigs to paint with, or paint with a leaf.

Bonus idea

Stand under a tree and look up into the branches. Can you follow a branch with your eyes until it forks, then choose the path you want to take and keep following until it branches again and again, until you finally reach the end of a twig reaching out to the sky? Follow the path back and start again, this time following a different path.

IDEA 72

Wind streamers

'You can always tell when it's windy outside as the children run around and get very excited by the weather.'

Investigate the power of the wind by making colourful streamers for running and dancing with.

It is important not to go into woodland areas in high winds because of the possibility of falling branches, but these are great opportunities to use an open space to experiment with this powerful force.

- Ask the children to find a stick each, at least the thickness of their thumb and the length of their forearm.
- Cut different colours of crêpe paper into long strips.
- Hold up a strip of masking tape horizontally and ask a child to stick the ends of the crêpe paper strips to it. Make sure that the strips are all hanging in the same direction. Four or five strips will be sufficient.
- Wrap the masking tape with the strips attached around one end of the stick. Have the crêpe paper facing outwards.
- You may want to add some more masking tape to the stick to make sure that the streamers are securely held in place.
- Let the children run, dance and wave their streamers to see the wind in action. Hold them up and let the wind blow; wiggle the sticks from side to side to make snakes; or make big arm loops to make streamer circles.

> **Bonus idea** ★
>
> Make flags from material or crêpe paper to complement this activity. Why not experiment with a team flag or one that represents your setting by gluing on leaves or crêpe paper cut-outs? Fix to sticks using masking tape or staple with a heavy-duty stapler directly onto the sticks, and place them in an exposed area to observe the direction that the wind is blowing in.

IDEA 73

Kites

'On windy days, our Forest School sessions are spent on the playing field, as we don't go into the woods.'

Continuing the theme of investigating the power of the wind, make simple kites for the children to fly on a breezy day.

Teaching tip

Children can practise their cooperation skills with this activity. They should ask a friend to hold the kite high in the air and then walk away from the kite, letting the string out behind them. Pull the string taut, and when there is a gust of wind, the person needs to launch the kite up into the air.

Woodlands can be dangerous when wind speeds are higher than Beaufort 5. Here's a quick rundown of the Beaufort scale:
- 0 – smoke rises vertically
- 1 – smoke drifts but leaves are still
- 2 – a light breeze and leaves rustle
- 3 – leaves and small twigs are constantly moving
- 4 – dust raised and small branches moving
- 5 – moderate-sized branches move and small trees sway
- 6 – large branches in motion, empty plastic bins blow over
- 7 – whole trees are in motion, difficult to walk.

For sessions spent on a playground or field because of the wind, why not make kites to fly?
- The simplest type is a vest-type carrier bag decorated with tissue paper shapes, with both the handles tied onto some light string – knitting wool or fishing line works well. Fill the bag with air and launch upwards.
- For a more sophisticated kite, split some willow rods or use wooden skewers but snip the point off, and form a cross shape. Use masking tape to hold it together.
- Stretch tracing paper, wax paper, tissue paper or ripstop nylon fabric over the sticks to form a kite shape. Hold in place with glue or masking tape.
- Make a tail by adding a ribbon or a strip of ripstop nylon.
- Tie a piece of string or fishing line to either end of one of the sticks and tie the flying string to the centre of this string.

Bonus idea ★

Why not try making a box kite or a wind sock-type kite? Decorate with tissue paper and have a mini kite festival.

IDEA 74

Experimenting with ice

'I can't believe it – I can melt ice with just my breath. I am like a dragon.'

Ice is a fascinating resource to explore outside. It is slippery, cold and it melts when handled. The children can be scientists as they experiment with the properties of ice and changing states.

If you know that it is going to be a cold night in advance, put out some containers of water in various shapes and sizes. If not, you can use ice found in puddles.

- Talk to the children about being scientific investigators. Ask them what they think ice is.
- Place the ice on a tray. Do they know what it is made of and what has happened to it? What does it feel like? Is it cold, slippery, sharp, dry, wet?
- Place a finger on the ice then put the finger on your neck. What does it feel like?
- What happens when you hold it in your hand? Give the children a straw each and ask them to blow on one area of ice each. What happens? Can they make a hole in the ice?
- What happens when you put the ice in a sunny spot?
- Can you stack pieces of ice into towers? Slightly dampen pieces of ice and press them together. Do they stick together and can you build a mini ice house from them?
- Experiment by sprinkling some table salt on the ice (little sachets are available from fast food cafés). What happens then?

Bonus idea ★

Freeze natural objects or plastic toys into ice and give children straws to blow hot breath to free the toys.

IDEA 75

Ice windows

'The children were fascinated today when ice formed on the puddles. We broke the ice and looked through it.'

This activity will demonstrate to children the transparency of ice and how it can be used to look through and freeze other objects.

Ice can make beautiful viewing windows to observe the changing seasons. They also glint and shimmer in the winter sunlight, making stunning natural mobiles.

- Before a cold night is forecast, gather some shallow containers such as baking trays.
- Find a level surface to put them on. Find natural materials such as leaves, pine cones, berries and small sticks.
- Tie a loop of string onto a stick and place it in the container so that the loop is hanging over the edges.
- Pour cold water into the container and make sure that all the natural objects are submerged.
- Leave it outside overnight. As long as the temperature is cold enough, the water will freeze. This can also be done in the freezer if the weather does not get cold enough.
- When frozen, gently remove the ice window from the container. You can warm the container with your hands or by blowing hot breath on it to release it from the container.
- Using the string loop, hang it up from a tree branch so that light glistens through the ice, and let the children observe what happens to it over the course of the session.

Taking it further

Once the container is prepared, add drops of different coloured food colouring to the water for a stained-glass effect. Do not move the tray or the colours will mix too much.

IDEA 76

Snow paths

'The children loved chugging around the track so much. This really hit the spot with our train-mad little boys.'

Getting out in all weathers is a key feature of the Forest School experience. In cold weather, it is important to keep the children moving so they do not chill too much. Snow paths are an exciting way to keep children busy and active.

Snow is my favourite type of weather. It transforms a familiar landscape into a fairy-tale scene, with a range of possibilities for using this new resource, from building snowmen to having ice cream pies in the mud kitchen. Take out buckets and spades to build snow castles or just for digging and transporting.

- If you have a reasonable snowfall, make a snow path.
- Start in an area blanketed in snow sufficient to cover the ground. Shuffle through the snow with your feet together to clear the snow away from the ground.
- Make a winding path for the children to follow. Are they being penguins, trains or racing cars? Maybe you could make a maze for them to follow.
- When they have tried out your track, show the children how to make their own and extend the path layout. Make crossroads, roundabouts and junctions.
- You can also make leaf paths in autumn, when the ground is covered in fallen leaves, using the same method.

Teaching tip

When the weather is cold, keep the children moving when outside and make sure they have lots of layers of clothes on. Check that the children don't get too cold when out in the snow. Their cheeks will be cold, but if you put your finger on their neck, just below the collar, it should feel warm.

Bonus idea ★

Bring some teddy bears to your Forest School session and talk to children about how bears hibernate during the winter. Build a warm, snug ice cave for the teddy bears to sleep in.

Part 8

Wildlife

IDEA 77

Animal ears

'How do I get the children to focus on sounds? My children just call out every time they hear anything!'

Showing children how to be quiet when outside can open up the chances of seeing some wildlife in your Forest School area.

Exploring the ways that animals move and listen can be an effective way to encourage children to focus on the sounds in their natural environment.

- Ask children to point at the sound. Stomp around, rustling leaves and cracking twigs. If they were little animals, would they come out to see what it was or would they hide until the danger was gone?
- Demonstrate how to move quietly, putting one foot slowly in front of the other. Place the heel down first and then put the weight on the side of the foot until your weight is on the whole foot.
- Practise being slow and quiet.
- Listen to the sounds around you. Cup your hands around your ears to show them how animals such as foxes and rabbits listen out for danger.
- Although human ears are fixed to hear sounds from in front of us, many animals can change the direction of their ears. Show the children how to cup their hands around their ears, with their little finger and the side of their hand in front of their ears, to amplify the sounds behind them.
- Cupping hands, palms upwards, underneath the ear can focus sounds from above, so if you are under a tree, you can hear birds and insects in the canopy more easily.

Teaching tip

Rather than immediately sharing every sound, ask children to hold up a finger for each different sound that they hear, until they get to five.

Bonus idea ★

If a woodland creature cannot hear you (because, of course, you are being so quiet), but they pop their head out of their hole, what do you think the animals would say seeing lots of humans? Why not change your shape and make your body more 'animal-like'? Bend over to make your body smaller, put your arms out to the side to look like wings or move differently by swaying, creeping and slithering.

IDEA 78

Animal games

'We surprised a rabbit sitting near the fire pit when we arrived this morning. One of the children said, "It's an elephant!" . . . well, it was grey and had big ears. We are going to learn some animal names!'

If you've never seen a rabbit before, how will you know what one is? Here are a couple of games to extend children's knowledge of animals.

Use photographs rather than cartoon pictures to learn the names of new animals, and talk about their features, habits and habitats.

Who am I?

- Collect together a range of pictures of animals, birds and insects that can be found in woodland habitats and mount them onto card. Laminate them for longevity.
- One of the children can pick a picture from the pack, and the others have to work out what is on the picture by asking questions.
- You may need to prompt the child with the card with suitable clues to give, such as 'I can fly', 'I like to come out at night', 'I like to eat mice' and 'I say "hooooo"'.

Scampering squirrels

- The next game is played like 'Simon says', but children have to sort fact from fiction.
- The leader asks the children to imitate an animal if the statement is true but do nothing if it is untrue. For example, 'horses trot, frogs jump, rabbits fly . . . no, rabbits jump, caterpillars wiggle, owls swim . . . no, it's fish that swim, owls fly'.
- This game can be used as a fun warm-up and also to check previous learning.

Teaching tip

Use the cards made for 'Who am I?' when learning about habitats. Use them on a rope-bus safari (see Idea 6) or to look at when making craft objects, such as pine cone hedgehogs (see Idea 79).

Taking it further

Who am I? is a good game for young children and can be revisited on subsequent sessions with new cards added in, to make sure that the more able children are stretched whilst the younger children can still enjoy the repetition and predictability.

IDEA 79

Pine cone hedgehogs

'We saw a hedgehog at Forest School. It was under the log pile. When Sally took some wood from the pile it came out and looked at me, then it walked away.'

Hedgehogs are fascinating yet elusive creatures, and often feature in children's storybooks, so when you do spot one it can be a magical moment for all. Making your site hedgehog-friendly, by making sure you have log piles, compost heaps and cosy corners for them to hide in, can increase the possibility of seeing one.

Hedgehogs weigh about 700 g and can live for up to five or six years. They like to eat lots of slugs and snails, and can travel up to 2–4 km each night foraging for food. They are nocturnal and they like to be by themselves rather than with other hedgehogs. A hedgehog hibernates from about November until March. Its body temperature in hibernation drops and it almost stops breathing.

- To make a hedgehog, cover a pine cone with clay. Push in pine needles to make the hedgehog's spines.
- Shape the clay to form a nose and make eyes by either adding small balls of clay or finding small stones or seeds to use as eyes.
- Make a warm nest with leaves for the hedgehog to sleep in.
- If pine cones are in short supply, you could make some hedgehogs using horse chestnut cases. Use a half shell of a horse chestnut casing (conker). Make the hedgehog's head and legs with some air-drying clay. Add small beads or seeds as eyes and a nose.
- If you have access to both pine cones and horse chestnut cases, you can make a hedgehog mother, who is called a sow, and her babies, who are called hoglets.

Teaching tip

This activity can be complemented by stories about hedgehogs. Our favourite stories are *The Winter Hedgehog* by Ann and Reg Cartwright and *Hedgehog Howdedo* by Lynley Dodd.

Bonus idea ★

You can also make hedgehog pictures by making a template of a hedgehog on some card. Cut it out and stick pointy leaves and twigs all over it to represent its prickles. If you hole-punch the card at the top before you start sticking, you can hang these up in the classroom to display or make a hedgehog mobile.

IDEA 80

Animal tracks

'We found some footprints near the fire pit today. We looked in Jordan's book and found out it was a fox that made them!'

This activity is one that you need to be prepared to do when the opportunity arises. It will lead to research and investigations by the children, comparing the prints with track guides to identify the animal that has left the print.

Finding animal trails is a good way of finding out who visits your Forest School site when you are not there. Not having an immediate answer for children but saying 'let's find out' is a good strategy for demonstrating to children how to extend their own knowledge by showing them where to look for information, rather than always supplying an answer.

- Preserve animal tracks by making a cardboard cylinder large enough to surround the footprint and pressing it into the ground around the print.
- An adult needs to measure out water into a mixing container and then sprinkle on some plaster of Paris powder. One cup of water should equal two cups of plaster of Paris. Tap the sides of the container to release any air bubbles and then keep adding the powder. The mixture will get hot. Stir the mixture until it is a smooth consistency, stand for a few minutes and then gently and slowly pour it into the card cylinder.
- Leave until the plaster is fully set then remove the card cylinder and lift out the footprint plaster. Use a paintbrush to brush away any loose soil.
- Make a collection of different footprints and compare them to each other. Look out for a range of mammals and birds, as well as different boot marks. You may want to make a human footprint for comparison.

Teaching tip

There are lots of books available for identifying animal trails. You can also visit the Woodland Trust website 'Nature Detectives' to print out identifying sheets.

IDEA 81

Stone and leaf animals

'I found a little nut, which has been nibbled by a mouse or it might have been a Gruffalo!'

Learning how to identify a range of local wildlife can stand the children in good stead for when they see an animal in real life. Making models of different creatures can also help the children to compare and contrast the different features.

Exploring the types of wildlife that may live in your woods helps children to build concepts of zoology and environmental stewardship to help them look after the natural world. Engaging children at a young age may influence future decisions about environmental planning many years from now – all because you had a hand in fostering a love for caring about wildlife in a small child at nursery.

- Talk to the children about the types of animals that might live in the woods. How many do they know? Extend children's knowledge by showing them pictures of different indigenous wildlife, and ask them if they know what they are, where they live and what they might eat.
- Look around your area and see what natural resources you can find. Make an animal from stones and pebbles. If on the beach, the addition of seashells can be very effective.
- Balance small stones on top of larger ones to make a relief sculpture, or lie them flat on the ground. Use leaves, grasses, lichen and sticks to add on features such as tails, ears, wings and legs.
- You can use chalks or charcoal to add in details such as pupils in the eyes, or nostrils on the nose. (Have wet wipes handy to clean up or, alternatively, you can make the rule that you can only use materials that you can find!)

Bonus idea ★

Take a photograph of one of these animals, then change the scene slightly and take another one. Keep doing this until the 'animal' has changed position. Back in the classroom, you could use technology to make a stop-motion animation of the moving animals, or print out the pictures and make them into a flip book.

IDEA 82

Fluffy owlets

'We have an owl which lives in our woods and we found some owl pellets. We soaked one in hot water and pulled it apart to discover what the owl had been eating and we saw some bones and fur. The children were fascinated by the whole process.'

If you are lucky enough to have your Forest School site within an owl's territory, you may be able to hear it calling out to other owls in the area. Making some baby owlets can support classroom learning about these beautiful birds.

Mother owl incubates the eggs while the father owl hunts to provide the food. When the owlets are larger and can maintain their own body temperature, the mother also hunts for food. When owls are little, they are fluffy with big eyes.

- To make your own owlet, find a pine cone. If it is warm and dry, the pine cone will open; you may need to dry out pine cones prior to this activity.
- Secure the stalk end of your pine cone on a small piece of clay to balance it upside down. Dab glue into the open leaves of the pine cone.
- Find a small stick and poke fluffed-up cotton wool into every gap. The addition of a couple of googly eyes – either the type you can get in a craft shop or stickers – and a beak will complete your owlet.
- How about making a home for your owlet in the hollow of a tree?

Taking it further

Look out for the lovely owl story to share, *Little Owl's Egg* by Debi Gliori. You can use the pine cone owlets to act out the story and really bring it to life.

IDEA 83

Birds' nests

'One of our parents found an empty nest which had fallen from a tree, and brought it to the nursery. The children were fascinated to look at it and it led to a deep discussion about how the birds manage to make the nests with their tiny beaks.'

The process of making a bird's nest can help children to appreciate just how much effort the parent birds put into keeping the eggs safe, and you could relate it to how their own parents and adults make sure that they are in a safe environment until they are big enough to start exploring their world.

Birds make their nests in different locations according to the species. Many birds make their nests in trees, bushes and off the ground, like blackbirds, chaffinches and crows. Swallows, house martins and song thrushes use mud and clay in theirs. Some birds make their nests in hollows in trees, such as owls and woodpeckers, while others, especially wading birds, build their nests on the ground.

- Talk with the children about how important it is for birds to build nests that keep the chicks safe and warm until they are ready to fly. Nests also need to be designed so that the egg doesn't roll out.
- Help the children to select suitable materials to build their nests, and find a location to put them. What will they need to keep the chicks warm while the parents fly off to find food for them?
- Can the nest be supported in the fork of a tree to keep it off the ground and away from predators?
- Try out the nests once finished by putting an egg inside. Does it roll about, will it fall out or is it safe? I have a collection of bird finger puppets to pop into the nests, which are available from educational catalogues and toy shops.

Involving parents

If you have some parents or grandparents who love knitting, there are lots of bird patterns available online and in knitting books.

Taking it further

Make some birds from air-drying clay decorated with feathers. If you use a V-shaped stick inside the clay as a scaffold, the head is less likely to fall off and cause disappointment.

IDEA 84

Festive bird garlands

'The children at our nursery are very nurturing to the birds that visit our setting and often build them nests. It is coming up to Christmas and some of the children have decided that the birds will be lonely when the nursery is closed for the holiday.'

Sharing celebrations with others and making your Forest School area more festive is lovely for promoting empathy and caring for others.

Talk to the children about who may visit your Forest School area when the children are not there, and prepare some surprise gifts for the local wildlife.

- Make some plain popcorn over the fire (see Idea 26 for instructions).
- Thread some strong thread onto plastic cross-stitching needles.
- You will initially need to support the children to show them how to use the needle safely.
- Carefully thread on popcorn, interspersed with cranberries, blueberries and multigrain hoops breakfast cereal, to make a festive garland. You can add in slices of dried orange if you wish.
- Hang the garlands from trees, ready for the birds to have an amazing Christmas dinner.
- After the garlands have been eaten by the birds, remove the threads from the trees.
- Children may want to make short strings of popcorn garlands, maybe 20–30 cm long, which you can then tie together to make long ones; or tie the ends of short lengths together to make individual circles to hang like mini wreaths.

> **Bonus idea** ★
>
> Once the birds' dinner is sorted, you may want to prepare dinner for the mice and squirrels in your area too. Choose some large leaves to be dinner plates and ask the children where they would like to place their offerings. Arrange some popcorn and cranberries and maybe add some nuts and seeds onto the 'plates' if allergies are not an issue.

IDEA 85

Orange bird feeders

'We have made a couple of half coconut shells to hang in the trees for the birds but it was not really a suitable activity for children to make.' Teacher, Exeter

If you enjoy freshly squeezed orange juice, this is a simple activity for using the shells to make a bird feeder.

Using orange shells is an easy and accessible way for children to make their own bird feeders.

- Cut some oranges in half and squeeze out the juice. Do not be worried about leaving some of the pulp inside the shells, as the birds enjoy this too.
- Give each child a half shell to make their own bird feeder.
- Make two holes in the sides of the orange shell and tie on a length of string to make a loop.
- In a bowl, cut up a packet of lard (or vegetable lard) into small pieces and beat with a wooden spoon until it is soft and smooth. As an alternative, you can also use the solid fat left in the tray from your Sunday roast (do not use this if you have vegetarian families in your setting).
- Mix in bird seed (wild bird seed is available from supermarkets and garden centres).
- Put some mixture into each orange shell and press in using spoons.
- Leave to harden, then hang from twigs and branches as a special treat for the birds in winter.

Involving parents

If you would like the children to take the bird feeders home, to share a bird-watching experience with their families, place on a tray to take back to nursery and pop into the fridge. Prior to taking home, brush some cling film with cooking oil and wrap the bird feeder to prevent the seeds escaping on the way home.

Bonus idea ★

You can use the same mixture to make pine cone bird feeders. Tie a string around the stalk of a pine cone and, using lollipop sticks, spread the mixture over the pine cone, making sure that the fat and seeds are poked into the crevices. Hang from branches and feed the birds.

IDEA 86

Apple bird feeders

'We have a child who is allergic to seeds and nuts, so bird feeders are not possible for our Forest School sessions.'

It is important to have alternative ideas so that all children can participate in activities. Fruit bird feeders are great for when you want to encourage birds to your area, and these make great presents to take home to hang in gardens.

Birds also like eating fruit during the winter months, and this is a great alternative treat for the birds.

- Cut some fresh hazel poles and lay on the ground.
- Help the children to use a pair of loppers to cut a stick about 3 cm thick and 20–25 cm long.
- Using a hand drill or a battery drill, make a hole about 2 cm in from each end of the stick.
- Use an awl or the drill bit to make the start of a hole in the centre of the stick. This is a guiding hole.
- Choose a screw at least 8 cm long and, using a screwdriver, go through the guiding hole and screw through the pole until the head of the screw is flush with the wood.
- Thread a piece of string about 75 cm long through both of the outer holes on the stick and knot the ends. Make sure that the middle screw is pointing upwards when the stick is hanging from the string.
- Carefully screw an apple onto the pointed end of the screw and hang the stick from a branch.
- You can reuse the bird feeder by putting on another apple when the first one has been eaten.

Teaching tip

A simpler version of this is to remove the core of an apple using a corer. Tie a piece of string to the centre of a stick and thread it through the hole made in the apple to hang it up.

Bonus idea ★

Why not make several stick feeders and run an experiment with the children? Screw a range of different fruit and vegetables onto the sticks and observe which ones the birds prefer to eat. You may want to use an apple, a carrot, a pear and a potato. Record your findings and discover the favourite bird food at Forest School.

Adventures of the imagination

Part 9

IDEA 87

Dinosaur bone hunt

'We have got lots of children in our setting who are dinosaur-mad; this activity totally engaged them for a whole session, searching for, collecting, arranging and transporting the bones around the woodland.' Nursery Manager, Cornwall

When dinosaur fever hits your nursery setting, dinosaur activities do not have to be confined to the art table or sand tray. Take the children's enthusiasm outdoors and set up some exciting adventures at Forest School.

Finding a topic that the children are truly enthusiastic about makes learning easy and engaging. This activity will spark imagination and keep them talking about their adventures for a long time.

- Buy some dinosaur bone sand moulds online, grease them with some cooking oil, prepare some plaster of Paris and pour it into the moulds. When dry, paint them a pale yellow and add a clear varnish.
- Hide the 'dinosaur bones' around your outside area. Sprinkle with soil and leaf debris.
- Give the children some palaeontologist's equipment, such as dinosaur ID sheets, trowels, chunky paintbrushes (to brush away the soil from the bones), magnifying glasses, hard hats and goggles.
- Show them the area where you suspect they might find some fossils (perhaps you 'found' one previously that you could show them!).
- Talk about the work of palaeontologists and how they have to carefully search for fossils. Demonstrate moving soil and brushing off the debris to expose the bones.
- Spread out a cloth for the children to display their finds and get ready to set up your own dinosaur museum.

Teaching tip

Talk to the children about the different types of dinosaurs and how and what they eat. See if they can find stones that could be carnivore teeth (sharp and pointy) or herbivore teeth (smoother and flatter). This learning can later be transferred to identifying the eating habits of other animals still around today.

Bonus idea ★

Use egg moulds (used by makers of candles and bath bombs), paint the eggs in different colours and varnish to preserve. Why not make a dinosaur egg nest or ask the children to build a nest for the eggs? Other activities could include making dinosaur footprints for children to follow and making dinosaur dinners (specifically for herbivores!).

IDEA 88

Salt dough leaf fossils

'A parent showed us their collection of fossils recently and the children were very interested; this has led to a whole prehistoric theme. We would like to take this further and make some fossils for the nursery.'

Many children are interested in dinosaurs and prehistoric times. One way to get a hands-on experience of prehistory is to share fossils with children, as they show us what life on Earth was like before there were people to tell us about it. Fossils leave a lasting impression (get it?).

Taking the prehistoric theme further, you can make some fossils to complement your dinosaur bones.

- To make your own fossils, you will need to mix two cups of flour and one cup of salt into a bowl.
- Slowly mix in up to one cup of water, with some food colouring of your choice, and mix until you have a firm dough. You will probably not need all of the water.
- Knead the dough and divide it into individual balls. Keep the salt dough moist by keeping it in a plastic lidded container.
- Find a leaf with defined veins and ridges. Slightly flatten the salt dough ball and press the leaf into the dough (vein-side down). Carefully remove the leaf and have a close look at the leaf impression.
- Place it onto a tray. You can make a hole at the top of the dough to hang it if you would like to make these into hanging ornaments or pendants. If it is a hot, dry day, these will harden in the sun; otherwise, when you return to nursery, place them in the oven on a very low heat or near a radiator to dry out.
- Try making fossils with a range of natural materials, such as sticks, lichens, snail shells, nuts and seeds.

> **Bonus idea** ★
>
> If you can find empty snail shells in your area, you can make some salt dough snails.

IDEA 89

Story stones

'We use these resources again and again both for Forest School sessions and in the nursery. We have quite a collection now and add to them to reflect the children's ideas.'

Sequencing stories or story starters can help children to structure events in literacy. These simple resources can be customised to cover the wide range of interests of the children, both in the classroom and outdoors.

Stories around the fire at Forest School can take on a whole new dimension with story stones. The children will be learning about sequencing, turn-taking, developing their imagination and storytelling skills, as well as speaking and listening and improving their vocabulary.

- You may want to prepare the stones before the session or children can paint one each.
- On each stone, paint a picture – keep it simple! Ideas could be plants, weather, people, a fire, a variety of wildlife or anything else that inspires you. Paint pictures of tools or favourite places at Forest School for a truly free-flow, personalised storytelling session.
- Put the stones in a bag and start telling a story. Each person takes it in turns to add to the story. They need to take a stone out of the bag and incorporate the picture in their tale.
- For a more structured approach, paint different characters from a well-known story on the stones – for instance, three bears, Goldilocks, bowls, chairs and beds – and use them to help children sequence the story. For a themed day, you may want the children to find stones that you have previously hidden around the site, bring them all together and try to guess the story; for instance, a mouse, a nut, a snake, an owl and a fox could lead into a Gruffalo hunt.

Teaching tip

As well as paint and permanent marker pens, you can also use cut-outs of pictures to stick onto the stones or, if you print pictures onto wax paper, you can transfer the images by laying the image face down on the stone and pressing it firmly all over with your fingers. Spray or gently brush with varnish to seal.

IDEA 90

Barefoot walk

'I had to walk in the mud and it went in my toes and it made lots of squelchy, squelchy noises. Then Sam had to clean my feet 'cos I had mud in my toes. It tickled.'

Set up a sensory experience for children to explore the sense of touch with their feet. This can be a challenging experience for some children, but one they will remember and talk about for a long time.

Walking barefoot helps to make children more aware of their surroundings, improves their balance and helps their posture.

- You will need to have access to water or wet wipes after this activity, especially if walking through mud. Do not do this activity in tick-infested areas.
- Carefully check the area prior to the activity for sharp objects, litter and animal faeces.
- Remove shoes and socks. Slowly walk through different terrains for a sensory experience outside. Examples of terrains to experience include wet grass, smooth pebbles, crunchy leaves, mud, sand, puddles and shallow streams.
- Talk to the children about their expectation and then their experience. Did each area feel like they expected?
- Talk to the children and support them when necessary while they are undergoing the barefoot walk.
- If your outdoor area does not have a range of terrains, why not set up your area to encompass them? Tuff trays or tarpaulins work well. To extend this activity further, why not ask the participants to close their eyes and lead them through the area or let the children lead the adults?

Taking it further

Link this activity with the story *We're Going on a Bear Hunt* by Michael Rosen. Why not end the experience with a teddy bear hiding in a fabric bag? Children can put their hands into the bag without seeing what is inside, so they can feel and guess who they have found.

Bonus idea ★

After walking through the muddy area, you could ask the children to stand on a piece of card to make muddy footprints.

IDEA 91

Smelly trails

'A police officer and his dog came to visit preschool and we learnt about how the police dog uses its sense of smell to follow a trail.'

Promoting the sense of smell is often neglected in Early Years activities, although it can be used to help children understand more about the world around them.

Using a smelly trail with children is a great way to explore the sense of smell as well as learning how animals can track their prey.

- Collect together some smelly things. Fruit or vegetables with a distinct smell are great – for instance, onion, garlic or oranges. You will need a cloth for each fruit or vegetable being used. You can also use things like peppermint essence.
- Send an adult or two ahead to lay the scent trails. Make sure you rub the smelly object – for instance, a strong-smelling onion cut in half to release the juices – onto trees as you go. Keep rubbing every metre or so. Lead each smell to a different part of your 'home base'.
- Rub the onion or the smell that the children are tracking onto a square of cloth. Let the children smell it before they set off so they can match the smell.
- If you lay another trail, use a contrasting smell – for instance, an orange has a very different smell from an onion – and do not let the two (or more) scents taint each other by keeping them well apart.
- At the end of the trail, let the group find their smelly source – had they worked it out along the way?

Taking it further

If the next activity you are going to do needs the group to be split into two, then at the start of the smelly trail allow alternate children to smell alternate cloths. You will hopefully have sorted groups at the end of the activity!

Bonus idea ★

Another way to divide a group into smaller ones by smell is to dab some perfumed oil onto the back of each child's hand. You can also use cloth or cardboard with some scent on if you have children with sensitive skin. Let the children smell each other's hands to see if they can find others with the same smell as them.

IDEA 92

Forest pets

'We have got a very nurturing group of children, who play with dolls and cuddly toys in the classroom. We don't like taking these into the forest as they get muddy.' EYFS Practitioner, Cornwall

These are fun activities, and the children initiating their own games involving animistic play around these resources have possibly been some of the cutest activities I have observed.

Promote caring and nurturing, as well as taking responsibility for others, by making pets at Forest School to promote lots of child-led play.

- Scatter some logs around your area for the children to find (ideally no longer than a child's forearm from wrist to elbow, and about the diameter – or maybe a little bigger – of the forearm).
- Ask the children to find themselves a log that they like the look of.
- Let the children decorate their log by drawing a face on one end with marker pens or charcoal, although this does not tend to remain on the log for long if the ground is damp.
- They then need to give their log a name. Show the children how to tie knots so that they can 'tie a lead' onto their log; elephant knots, clove hitches and good old granny knots work well.
- Take the pet log for a walk, build him a home, play with him or let him visit other logs in the area.
- If logs are scarce and you have a horse chestnut tree on your grounds, you may want to go on a conker hunt in autumn (always have a sneaky few spare ones in your pocket just in case anyone is unsuccessful).
- Decorate the conkers with felt feet, pompoms and googly eyes to make little characters to build homes for and look after.

Teaching tip

An alternative to googly eyes can be white stickers with black pupils drawn on them.

109

IDEA 93

Gold rush

'We found real gold at Forest School! We made a treasure pile and have hidden it under the tree to stop pirates from finding it. I'm going to tell my dad where it is though – he's not a pirate.'

Setting up an adventure for the children to experience can capture their imagination and initiate storytelling. A simple resource strategically placed in your Forest School area can promote a plethora of pretend play.

This activity can be used as it is or to support projects on a variety of subjects, including a history of the Gold Rush mining era, precious metals, treasure hunting and pirates, as well as promoting gross and fine motor skills, observational skills and sorting and collecting.

- Create a gold rush in your outdoor area. Collect, wash and dry small stones and pebbles. Spray paint them with gold paint and leave to dry. (Metallic spray paint is available in DIY stores, art and craft shops or online.) Make sure that the paint is non-toxic and encourage children to wash their hands after the activity.
- Put the gold pieces around your outdoor area, arm your children with collecting pots and let them find the pieces. This can be further extended by burying pieces of gold in fine soil or the sand pit and giving children sieves to hunt for the gold.
- How about a session panning for gold? Show the children how to scoop up a mixture of water, sand and gold bits onto a tin plate and, using a swirling motion, let the mud wash off until the heavier gold pieces are left behind.
- If you also prepare stones painted with silver and copper, you could then extend the activity into sorting.

> **Teaching tip**
>
> These activities fit in well with treasure hunts (add in some translucent gemstones of different colours, available from pet shops and garden centres) and can also be used for pirates, fairy treasures, silver or gold anniversaries and celebrations.

> **Bonus idea** ★
>
> Once the children have collected the treasure, they can use it to make trails in the Forest School area for each other. This activity complements stories such as Hansel and Gretel or pirate stories.

IDEA 94

Shadows

'The children love chasing and jumping on each other's shadows on sunny days. What can we do to support and extend this interest?'
EYFS Practitioner

On a bright, sunny day, these activities are great for exploring shadows and shade as well as mark-making.

The contrast of light and dark can be explored by looking at shadows. Shadows fascinate small children, and some can't quite believe their shadows do not have a mind of their own!

- Find an area where children can cast shadows on the ground and see what funny shapes they can make with their bodies.
- Ask a child to make a shape with their body, and the others need to 'paint' their shadow with a bucket of water and large paintbrushes. Alternatively, you could use squeezy bottles filled with water.
- When completed, you should see the child's shadow on the ground even when they move away.
- As this is a very temporary artwork, it is a good idea to capture the results on camera.
- For longer-lasting results, you can lay down some white paper on the ground; wall lining paper works very well.
- Use charcoal and mud to trace the outline of the shadow and fill in the shape with mud or natural objects such as leaves and twigs.
- If you want this to be a more permanent piece of work, use glue to stick on the leaves, etc. Decorate the body shape in Aboriginal style by using fingers and sticks as paintbrushes and mud and clay as paint.
- You can also try capturing the shadow of natural objects such as leaves, flowers and sticks or bigger objects such as trees and bushes.

Teaching tip

Ensure that you have hand-washing facilities available, as this is quite a muddy activity.

Taking it further

For a fine motor control activity, try the same method with toys and stencils. Cast their shadows onto paper on a clipboard, and use pencils to decorate. Toy plastic animals and even soft toys such as teddy bears cast great shadows when positioned correctly, and are a good aid to learning how to draw the shape of things accurately.

IDEA 95

Den building

'We had a den-building session at the beginning of term and they are still there. The children revisit them every session and add bits on or change the design every week. One of the dads said he had spent his weekend making a den in the garden with his daughter as she could talk of nothing else.'

Den building can spark children's imagination and promote lots of imaginative, child-initiated games. Children often plan, problem-solve and work cooperatively to build and improve their dens in subsequent sessions.

Teaching tip

At the end of each term, make sure that you dismantle the structures and remove any string from trees, as this can inhibit growth. Replace the wood around your area, to be found and utilised on other occasions.

- Help the children decide on an appropriate and safe spot to build their den (not near the fire area, nettles, brambles or in an area that could become too muddy in inclement weather).
- Help the children to lash some poles together or use the forks in trees to start the building.
- Use sticks and natural materials to build up the den.
- Check that the den is safe and nothing heavy will fall on the children once inside. Use string or paracord to make the den sturdy and stable.
- If your area does not have much in the way of building materials, think about contacting your local council (parks or highways departments) as they will often be happy to drop off or allow you to collect materials when they are tree-cutting.
- For temporary structures that are to be cleared away at the end of the session, you can also supply plastic tarpaulins (available from DIY and sometimes pound shops), large pieces of material and gardening canes if your council have nothing available.
- Make string readily available and offer mats or small tarpaulins to go inside the dens to make them cosy.

IDEA 96

Body art

'We made hand make-up with flowers and I had Batman. My mum would like Batman make-up but you are not allowed to do it on your face, so I will do it on her hand.'

Using decorations on our bodies is something that stretches back to ancient times. Tattoos are commonplace and face painting is something that most children will have experienced.

Mark-making does not need to be necessarily confined to paper but can be encouraged anywhere to promote a love of writing and art. Body painting can help children to understand other cultures, such as Mehndi hand painting or tribal art.

- Check for allergies. Ask children not to draw on their faces, as parents may not be happy about it. I ask them to limit designs to the back of their hand or lower forearm only.
- Pick a fresh dandelion, including the stalk. Use the white sap from the flower stalk to draw a tattoo design onto your skin. This will develop over several hours to be light brown, and last a couple of days depending on washing activity.
- Mud mixed with some water is also great to use. Spread over the back of the hand and, using a finger or a non-sharp stick, draw a pattern or picture in the mud and allow it to dry.
- Make nail polish with mud and use a paintbrush to apply it to fingernails.
- Charcoal from the fire makes bold black marks. Either use it as it is or crush it with a pebble on a stone, like a mortar and pestle, and mix it with a little water then apply using fingers or brushes.
- With mud and charcoal, if you are not happy with the design, wash it off and start again.

Bonus idea ★

Using a soft, pliable leaf, make a template (for instance, a bat silhouette) using scissors and place it on the back of the hand. Stipple mud mix over the template with a handful of grass made into a brush. Carefully remove the leaf and leave to dry.

IDEA 97

Gross motor playground

'When we get to the Forest School area, the children all line up to use the rope swing. It is their favourite bit and everyone needs a go before we can start other activities.'

Rope swings are wonderful fun but, rather than waiting for a turn, why not make your whole area into an outdoor playground?

Letting children design and build their own adventure playground means that everything is customised to their needs and wants, and can be improved and altered as their abilities (and challenge levels) change.

- Make a climbing area by putting large logs in one area. Make sure that the ground is reasonably clear of forest-floor debris that could damage a child if they fell off a log.
- Introduce some planks to balance between the logs. Make them short and moveable so the children can work cooperatively to build their own configuration.
- Make a rope bridge by tying a rope around a tree. Wind it round about four times and pull tight. Stretch the rope to another tree and tie it so that you have a horizontal rope about shin height off the ground.
- Tie another rope at child head height from the ground and parallel to the first one. Use sit mats or carpet squares to protect the trunk of the tree and stop the rope rubbing the bark away. The children can walk along the rope using the higher rope for support. I use a variety of ropes but the blue plastic variety available from DIY stores works fine. It is sometimes worth talking to climbing centres, as they have to check and replace their ropes regularly.
- Slack lines are reasonably cheap in the European-style supermarkets on occasion, and work well as rope bridges.

Teaching tip

Ask the children to share their ideas about what they would like to use, and work out together how it can be achieved.

Taking it further

If you have a slope with a clear landing area, make a mud slide on damp days by using heavy duty sacks or a tarpaulin.

IDEA 98

Forest School in the dark

'The children love going out after dark. It adds an extra dimension to their Forest School adventure.' Forest School Leader, Plymouth

Everything looks different in the dark. Shadows look like doorways into other worlds, bright colours become muted to greys and a familiar area becomes a new place to explore.

When the days grow short, take the opportunity to hold Forest School after dark. Wrap up warm and go on an adventure. These activities are also great for family camps and events.

- Use hand held torches or head torches for a bug hunt. Many minibeasts who hide away during the day are busy at night. Look on tree bark and under rocks and logs.
- Hang a white sheet between two trees and shine a powerful torch at it. Moths will land on the sheet so that the children can inspect them and maybe compare them to observations from butterflies they have seen during the day time.
- Make a trail for children to follow using luminous stickers on pebbles or trees. When they shine their torches, the stickers will glow making them easy to find and follow.
- You can buy luminous paint and decorate some pebbles prior to the session to make a trail or mark out paths.
- Play stalking in the dark. Give one child a torch. They need to switch it off and close their eyes. Start the other children in a wide circle around the perimeter of your area. When the torch is off, they need to slowly creep to the centre. If the child hears a noise they must point the torch at the sound and switch it on. Anyone caught in the beam is frozen. When the light is switched back off again the children continue creeping forward until someone reaches the centre.

Teaching tip

When walking in the dark with children, use a rope bus to help them feel more secure or put a hand on the shoulder of the person in front to make a train. If you want to be able to spot children easily in the dark, then road safety waistcoats or reflective strips attached to coats can help.

Taking it further

Make play-in-the-dark skittles by popping some glow sticks into empty plastic bottles and using a luminous ball to knock them down with. Hoopla is also a great game; make hoops from glow sticks and throw them over the skittles or luminous painted sticks.

Bonus idea ★

Prepare the fire area before dark and light it when you get there for an unforgettable story telling session around the fire.

115

IDEA 99

The unplanned adventure

'It's just like a holiday!'

Some of the nicest sessions are those that are totally unplanned and where the prepared resources do not even make it out of the bag.

Teaching tip

Don't! The adult's role is to observe, join in when invited and supply resources when required.

Unplanned adventures still need planning! Make sure you always have your bag with an emergency kit (spare clothing, a first aid kit and a telephone for emergencies).

- In my rucksack, along with the essentials above, I also carry a few resources just in case the children need things to make their ideas possible. This includes a camera, a ball of string, scissors, pens, a small knife, a couple of small, plastic tarpaulins, some zip top sandwich bags and a folding saw.
- Make sure that the children and staff are dressed for whatever the weather can throw at you and let the children lead the way.
- Children have initiated games such as bear hunts, hide and seek, den building, making traps for pirates, princesses, mummies and daddies, explorers, knights, superheroes, going to the beach (there were a lot of puddles!), sailing stick boats and being a tribe of fairies who had their own language.
- As a child, many of us were given freedom to just play – and, in fact, this constitutes some of our happiest memories as children – but often these days a child's day is organised and planned to optimise the learning objectives and hit adult-imposed targets. Sometimes, stepping back and letting children initiate their own play is of more use to their deep-level learning, memory-building, problem-solving, and social and emotional development than a session with a lesson plan.

IDEA 100

Reviewing the session

'When the children arrive back at the nursery after a session, they are happy but tired. We know it has been a successful experience for them, but they are talking about something seen on the walk back, something in the playroom or what might be for lunch.'

At the end of the session, it is important to review with the children what they have done. This helps them reflect and can remind them what they have achieved during the session and show that it was a valued experience.

Gather the group together at the end of the session and settle everyone around the rope-bus circle before you start.

- Talking about the session while it is still fresh in their minds – what went well or what they would do differently – helps build strategies when faced with a similar challenge in the future, as well as reassures them that it is okay to take risks and fail sometimes too.
- Sessions can have so many elements to them, so it is useful to remind the children of all the things they have done.
- Pose questions such as 'Did you like splashing in the puddles?' or 'Who liked the slimy slugs?'. Ask for a thumbs up or down response.
- Have a talking stick, puppet or toy for the child to hold while talking. They can express both positive and negative thoughts, so pose questions like 'What was the best/funniest/proudest bit?' or 'What was the worst/scariest/wettest bit?'.
- How about praising each other by saying what made them proud about other children in the group? Other children will praise qualities and abilities that perhaps individuals would not see in themselves.

Teaching tip

Sing a song to the tune of 'Here we go round the mulberry bush': 'What did we do at Forest School, Forest School, Forest School, What did we do at Forest School on a warm and sunny morning?' (Or a cold and rainy afternoon as appropriate!) Continue with 'This is the way we sharpened sticks, made some bugs, drank hot chocolate, collected leaves' and so on.

Bonus idea ★

Make a stick or tree cookie with a happy face and a sad face on it for the child to match their response with their thoughts. The children can decorate these themselves.

Further reading

Hodgeson, J. and Dyer, A. (2003), *Let Your Children Go Back to Nature*. Milverton: Cappal Bann.

Maciver, T. (2013), *Activities, Games and Challenges for Learning Outside the Classroom*. Consultancy Education Forest: Exeter, UK.

Community Woodland Network, www.communitywoodland.org.

EYFS Statutory Framework, www.foundationyears.org.uk.

Forest School and Outdoor Learning, www.forestschoolandoutdoorlearning.co.uk.

Forest School Association, www.forestschoolassociation.org.

Goldsworthy, A., Morning Earth, www.morning-earth.org.

I Love Forest School (Facebook page), https://www.facebook.com/groups/124568654451/.

Local Wildlife Trusts, www.wildlifetrusts.org.

TCV (conservation volunteers), www.tcv.org.uk.

The Field Studies Council, www.field-studies-council.org/publications.

The National Trust, www.nationaltrust.org.uk.

Woodland Trust, www.naturedetectives.org.uk.